THE HOME-BASED ENTREPRENEUR

by
LINDA PINSON
&
JERRY JINNETT

Published by

OUT OF YOUR MIND . . .
AND INTO THE MARKET PLACE™

THE HOME-BASED ENTREPRENEUR

By Linda Pinson and Jerry Jinnett

First printing: October, 1989

Published by: **OUT OF YOUR MIND....**
             AND INTO THE MARKETPLACE ™
                  13381 White Sand
                  Tustin, CA 92680
                  (714) 544-0248

Cover design by Linda Pinson

Library of Congress Catalog Card No: 89-091720

ISBN 0-944205-13-5 (8 1/2 x 11 paperbound)
Printed in the United States of America

INTRODUCTION

According to the American Home Business Association, there are 13 million full-time home businesses in the United States with another 14 million part-time corporate homeworkers or home-business owners. The AHBA projected that one million new home businesses would be launched in 1989. Their purchases of computer and software equipment, FAX machines, copiers, and other office equipment, supplies, and furniture should inject as much as $100 billion into the economy. The home-based business movement is indeed a business entity to be recognized.

The purpose of this book is to take a realistic look at that home-based movement. The feasibility of starting a business in one's home will be presented by looking at zoning, licensing, and legal concerns, by analyzing the advantages and disadvantages of a home office, and by evaluating the owner's skills, interests, and personality traits. The step-by-step format for business start-up will be covered along with insurance, finance, taxes, marketing, and advertising. Business Incubators will be discussed as an alternative location.

In 1988, half of all the companies that were less than 5 years old failed. The major reasons seemed to be inadequate cash flow, lack of business know-how, and poor management techniques. It is hoped that this book will decrease the risks of failure by presenting a realistic look at the business process. An extensive resource list is presented at the end of the book to help you gather the knowledge you will need to turn your idea into a successful home-based business.

Small Business Consulting
Textbooks
Seminars

TABLE OF CONTENTS

1. **HISTORY OF HOME-BASED BUSINESS** .... **1 - 4**

2. **ZONING, LABOR LAWS, AND LICENSES**...................... **5- 10**
   Zoning 7
   Labor Laws 9
   Business Licenses 10

3. **ADVANTAGES & DISADVANTAGES OF THE HOME OFFICE** **11-18**

4. **PERSONAL ASSESSMENT** **19-22**

5. **HOW TO FIND A BUSINESS** **23-28**

6. **STEPS TO STARTING A BUSINESS**........................... **29-38**
   Choose a Business Name 31
   Choose Your Legal Structure 33
   Obtain a Business License 35
   File Your DBA 36
   Obtain a Seller's Permit 36
   Set Up a Business Bank Account 37

7. **SUCCESS OR FAILURE: IT DEPENDS ON YOUR CASH FLOW** **39-54**
   What is a Cash Flow Statement? 41
   Pre-Planning Worksheets 42
   Building the Cash Flow Statement 48

8. **RECORDKEEPING FOR A HOME-BASED BUSINESS** **55-76**
   General Information 57
   General Records 60
   Financial Statements 62
   Recordkeeping Schedule 65
   Sample Forms 66

9. **TAX DEDUCTIONS FOR A HOME-BASED BUSINESS** **77-88**
   Home Business Use Test 79
   Deductions for Business Use of A Home 80
   Home Office Deductions Limitation 84

10. **INSURANCE CONSIDERATIONS** **89-92**

11. **MARKET RESEARCH** **93-98**
    Questionnaires 95
    Evaluation of the Competition 96
    Pricing Your Product or Service 97

12. BUSINESS VIABILITY:
COSTING/PRICING YOUR PRODUCT
OR SERVICE **99-108**
Cost of Your Product or Service 102
Selling Price 103
Putting Together a Picture of Your Business 103
Formulas - Hourly Rate & Manufacturers' 105

13. PROMOTING & ADVERTISING A
HOME-BASED BUSINESS **109-116**
Salesmanship 112
Publicity.. 112
Advertising 114

14. BUSINESS INCUBATORS **117-120**

15. RESOURCE GUIDE **121-161**
Small Business Administration 123
Other Federal Resources 126
State Resource Guide 128
Associations 156
Books & Publications 157
Library Resources 159
Personal Business Resource List 161

16. INDEX **163**

OTHER BOOKS

by

LINDA PINSON & JERRY JINNETT

1. OUT OF YOUR MIND...AND INTO THE MARKETPLACE

A step-by-step guide for starting and succeeding with a small or home-based business. Takes you through the mechanics of business start-up and provides you with an overview of information on such topics as copyrights, trademarks, and patents, legal structures, financing, and marketing.

2. ANATOMY OF A BUSINESS PLAN

Will enable you to research and write your own business plan. This book is designed to take away the mystery and help you to put together a plan that will both satisfy a lender and enable you to analyze your company and implement changes that will insure success.

AUTOMATE YOUR BUSINESS PLAN — See the reverse side of this page for our Business Planning Software description and order information.

3. MARKETING: RESEARCHING AND REACHING YOUR TARGET MARKET

A comprehensive guide to marketing your business. This book not only shows you how to reach your target market, but gives you a wealth of information on how to research that market through the use of library resources, questionnaires, etc.

4. RECORDKEEPING: THE SECRET TO GROWTH & PROFIT

Basic business recordkeeping both explained and illustrated. This book is excellent if you are new to business recordkeeping or if your records are in trouble. It is designed to give a clear understanding of small-business accounting by taking you step-by-step through general records, development of financial statements, tax reporting, the development of a recordkeeping schedule, and financial statement analysis.

These books are available through your bookstore or directly from the publisher, **OUT OF YOUR MIND...AND INTO THE MARKETPLACE™**

OUT OF YOUR MIND...AND INTO THE MARKETPLACE™
13381 White Sand, Tustin, CA 92680
(714) 544-0248

AUTOMATE YOUR BUSINESS PLAN!

WITH OUR SOFTWARE, YOU WILL BE ABLE TO:

- **Computerize your financial spreadsheets**
- **Use simple and flexible word processing templates to produce a quality business plan.**

Out of Your Mind and Into the Marketplace™ has combined with **Analytical Software Partners** to produce a business planning software package called "Automating A Business Plan". This automated tool will simplify your business planning process, applying the principles set forth in "Anatomy of a Business Plan". This software package runs on any standard IBM PC or compatible with 512 K of internal memory and a 360K floppy disk drive. It does not require any other supporting software package or spreadsheet program. In keeping with our simplified philosophy of business planning, the software is straightforward and easy to use. It requires no specialized computer background or study. As an added bonus it includes a full featured word processor which is both powerful and simple to use. "Automating A Business Plan" may be just the boost you need to quickly produce a professional quality business plan which puts you on the road to success. If you would like more details, write for a brochure or complete the order blank below and reserve your copy immediately!

WELL CONSTRUCTED SOFTWARE MAY BE THE SINGLE MOST IMPORTANT PRODUCTIVITY TOOL A NEW COMPANY CAN ACQUIRE. TIME IS <u>THE</u> KEY COMMODITY FOR START-UP BUSINESSES. AUTOMATION CAN STRETCH THIS CRITICAL COMMODITY. CAREFULLY CHOSEN SOFTWARE CAN MAKE YOUR PC A BUSINESS PARTNER RATHER THAN AN ADVERSARY!

ORDER TODAY
(JUST FILL IN THE ORDER BLANK BELOW)

☐ **Automating A Business Plan** _____
(Software Package) @ $79.00

☐ **Anatomy of A Business Plan &** _____
Automating A Business Plan
(Text & Software Package @ $95)

☐ California residents, _____
please add 6% sales tax.

☐ Shipping Fees $2.50 _____

☐ Next Day Air Express $15.00 _____

Total Amount Due $ _____

Prices Effective October 1989

Name_____

Address_____

City_____

State:_____ Zip Code:____

Make Check or Money Order Payable to:

OUT OF YOUR MIND ....
AND INTO THE MARKETPLACE™
13381 White Sand Drive
Tustin, CA 92680
(714) 544-0248

NOTE: WE WILL HAVE A MAC INTOSH VERSION ··· AVAILABLE JAN. 1990!

HISTORY OF
HOME-BASED
BUSINESS

THE HOME-BASED ENTREPRENEUR

HISTORY OF HOME-BASED BUSINESS

Home-based business is not a new phenomena. Until the 19th century, the world's economy was primarily agricultural. The majority of people lived on farms or in small villages. The farmers raised produce and livestock for their own use and to exchange for the goods and services of the craftsmen and professionals in the towns. Since the workers made the products in their homes or the service providers operated from home offices, this became known as the "domestic system".

The term "cottage industry" came into use during the Industrial Revolution. It began as a work arrangement between an entrepreneur and a worker. The entrepreneur supplied the raw materials and the worker created a finished product. Most often, the worker created the product in the home, worked independently, could accept or reject work, and was not considered an employee of the entrepreneur, but an independent contractor. The entrepreneur provided raw materials, paid for the work done, and was responsible for marketing and selling the goods. The Industrial Revolution of the 1800's was an evolutionary process and, initially, spurred large growth in cottage industry. For example, a machine which could spin thread was invented prior to the invention of weaving and sewing machines. More workers than ever were needed to turn the thread into cloth and turn the cloth into clothing. Great numbers of home workers were engaged in the clothing industry.

Factories of the early 1800's were small and crowded with poor working conditions and low wages. Much work continued to be sublet to the home workers. These poor conditions continued during and after the Civil War. Following the war, people began to protest the sweatshop conditions. With the formation of labor unions, workers gained the power and protection to improve their working conditions. In the early 1900's, union pressure led to laws prohibiting work outside factories. Better machines and assembly line production techniques led to a centralization of business. "Cottage industry" became uncommon and was relegated to secondary incomes and the pursuit of hobbies. Working from home was no longer looked upon as a legitimate or respected way of earning a living.

"Going to work" has described the economic situation since the later part of the Industrial Revolution. The concept that work takes place at a location away from home became the traditional view.

Over the past thirty years, the structure of our economy has changed from an industrial base to a service and informational base. During this time, small business began to increase its role and importance in the economy. Americans of all ages and economic backgrounds began starting, purchasing, and expanding small business throughout the country. Many of these businesses were based in the home.

We were entering the Electronic or Computer Revolution and were finding that the computer offered more freedom in the workplace. Work could be taken home to what Alvin Toffler calls the "electronic cottage". Futurist Jack Nilles coined the term "telecommuting". As we moved into the Electronic or Computer age, entrepreneurship was again gaining attention. The post-war baby boom has filled today's work force with many well-educated employees at a time when office automation, plant closings, and economic pressures have created fewer career advancement opportunities. Most two-parent families now need two incomes in order to survive. As a result, nearly two thirds of all mothers work for pay outside the home. This is a reversal from the 1950's when two thirds stayed home. Stress related illnesses of hypertension, chronic headache, heart disease, and alcoholism and drug abuse are on the increase.

Modern technology has made it possible for almost every family to start its own business at home. Parents are seeking work that will allow them to stay at home with their families. It is more economical to work at home than to rent or buy work space elsewhere. Home-based business is a way to avoid difficult and costly commuting. The handicapped are discovering working possibilities that enable them to stay at home. Job insecurities have forced white-collar workers to pile out of corporations. Factory shutdown from 1979 to 1984 caused 11 1/2 million Americans to lose their jobs. Only 60% had found work by 1987.

The rising cost of office space, fuel, and overhead coupled with an increase in job-related stress has led to a change of attitude on the part of big businesses. Many corporations have found it cost-effective to have employees "telecommute". They work at least part of the time from their homes, from which they are linked to the main office via computer terminals.

The home-office seems to be a perfect location for the new entrepreneur. Much is written that extols the promise of home-based work for all types of people: discontented employees, the unemployed, parents of young children, re-entry women, the retired, the handicapped, and tired commuters. By the mid 1980's, the push toward the home-office was in full swing. Home-based work seems to be the great panacea--the option which will solve all the problems of the workplace. But as the number of people working from home increases, pressure is rising for and against altering laws and regulations which affect the home office. Initial advantages of the home-office can quickly become disadvantages. A decision to have a home business should be an educated one. The major issues in the near future for home-based entrepreneurs will be zoning, labor laws, and licensing.

ZONING
LABOR LAWS
LICENSES

THE HOME-BASED ENTREPRENEUR

ZONING
LABOR LAWS
LICENSES

Most current zoning ordinances that restrict business use of the home arose from a desire to protect neighborhoods from the smokestacks of the Industrial Revolution. Many were written during or after the Civil War! While these laws are outdated and may not be appropriate to the times in which we live, violation is a crime and can be punishable by a fine and/or business closure.

Zoning ordinances vary widely and are created at the city or county level. Contact your city or county government to determine the department responsible for zoning.

Zoning ordinances divide a city or county into four basic classifications: Residential, Commercial, Industrial, and Agricultural. Residential zoning restrictions present the most problems for the home office. Most are aimed at insuring that the character of the neighborhood will not be changed in any way. The most common restrictions follow:

1. **No On-Site Sales** - The concern is that sales of merchandise from the home office will increase foot and vehicle traffic in the area, thus changing the character of the neighborhood. Many product oriented businesses use mail order or delivery services to get their goods to the customer and to satisfy the law. Service and professional businesses develop a mobile character and provide their work in the client's home.

2. **Space Limitations** - Often the percentage of total residential square footage which can be used for business will be designated. This can lead to creativity in designing your workspace. Closet organizers and modular furniture enable the owner to gain more usable space in a low square footage area.

3. **No deliveries** - Again, we have the concern of increasing traffic in a residential area. The owner may have to be responsible for picking up supplies.

4. **No storage of inventory** - This is a safeguard against on-site sales. There are also fire and safety considerations. Many home businesses store their inventory in mini-storage rental units away from the home site.

5. **Concern for pollution from noise, hazardous waste, and odors** - These ordinances are the most strictly enforced because violation will most certainly have an impact on the neighborhood. Contact the State Regulatory Agency with jurisdiction over these areas of concern and learn the safeguards to be used when working with hazardous materials or wastes. You may still be denied a business license for home use even though you can demonstrate a thorough knowledge of toxic material handling and disposal.

6. **No business signs** - No signs or other means of advertising may be placed in a residential area. This may also include signs on the vehicle used by your business. Some home business owners use magnetic signs which are attached to the vehicle when leaving the residential area in pursuit of business.

7. **Fire Hazard** - Often a fire department will have to inspect the premises and issue a permit if you work with flammable materials.

8. **No employees other than family members** - This restriction limits the growth of a home business. The owner is restricted to the amount of work he is able to perform. Owners may have to use contract labor: individuals who can work in their own locations without supervision and expand the work capability of the home office. This is also a viable alternative when no manufacturing is allowed in the home.

The zoning commission will be made aware of your business when you apply for a business loan, a sales tax permit, or a business license. Most often zoning violations are reported by unhappy or feuding neighbors. If you are charged with a violation, you will be sent a notice ordering you to stop business immediately or file an appeal. Ignorance of the law is no excuse.

It is good judgement to contact the Planning or Zoning Commission and obtain a copy of the zoning ordinance for your area. Know specifically what you can and cannot do and adjust your business accordingly. If your local zoning laws prohibit or severely restrict home business, work with the zoning commission to effect change through political action.

It is important to keep up-to-date with zoning legislation in your community. One way is to read local newspapers, especially the "neighborhood" sections. Be sure to notice items about such things as redevelopment or revitalization projects, proposed freeway or road changes, or new commercial developments. Changes such as these may influence the zoning in your area. Another way is to keep aware of trends and zoning issues by joining civic and business organizations , such as the Chamber of Commerce, Rotary Club, National Association of Women Business Owners, or the Business and Professional Women's Organization. Through your reading and networking, you will become aware of all the latest local and national news concerning home-based business.

LABOR LAWS

In addition to local zoning considerations, the home business owner must be concerned with legislation on the state and federal level. Only a few states have labor laws which specifically target work done in the home. Their purpose is to govern work which would normally be done in a factory under assembly line conditions. When such work is done at home it is termed "industrial home work" and may reflect a history of worker exploitation. State labor laws serve the purpose of guaranteeing worker safety and insuring that minimum wage requirements are met.

States which do not have labor laws fall under the U.S. Department of Labor. Its Fair Labor and Standards Act of 1938 initially prohibited seven industries from using home workers: knitted outerwear, gloves and mittens, belts and buckles, jewelry, women's apparel, embroidery, and handkerchiefs. The Second World War saw a retooling of factories in order to keep up the demands for products and munitions to supply the war effort. Enforcement of the FLSA was often relaxed in some regions and work in the prohibited areas of knitted outerwear and gloves and mittens began to be done in the home setting, on a piecework basis. The Industrial Work Act of 1943 reinforced the ban on specific areas of homework.

The right to work at home is being challenged in many states with laws and/or amendments to this act. The banned industries have been the subject of controversy and litigation in recent years as unions challenge the right to work at home. In December, 1984, the ban on knitted outerwear was lifted. The remaining six industries remain prohibited. Soon after the ban on knitted outerwear was lifted, Senator Orrin Hatch introduced the Freedom of the Workplace Act to remove the prohibitions of the FLSA. It called for a complete reversal of the FLSA restrictions on home work.

In October of 1983, the AFL-CIO passed a resolution calling for a ban on computer homework except in the case of the handicapped. They fear the development of an "electronic sweatshop".

Several labor unions feel that home-based business threatens the job security of their members and that some home-workers may be exploited. Some unions continue to apply pressure on Congress and state legislative bodies in order to place limits or bans on specific areas of home work.

As a home business owner, it is your responsibility to keep up-to-date on legal issues which may affect you or your business. Keep in touch with your state and national officials and representatives. Let them know your areas of concern and ask to be placed on their mailing lists.

BUSINESS LICENSES

Most cities have licensing requirements that will apply to you. If your business is to operate within the law, you must obtain a business license or permit in the city in which your business is located. If you reside in an un-incorporated area, the county often grants a business license or use permit. If your business is service-oriented and the service is performed in cities other than the one in which you have a business license, you may also be required to purchase permits from those cities to cover the time period in which you will be working in their areas. Business licenses provide cities with a source of revenue and a means of controlling the types of businesses which can operate within their jurisdictions.

A business license is inexpensive and lends credibility to your company. The business license bureau and zoning commission frequently work hand-in-hand. Often, approval from the zoning commission is a pre-requisite for getting a business license. Just as with the zoning commission, meet with a representative of the licensing department if you are turned down. Work through ways of satisfying the requirements and of operating within the law.

Certain businesses are subject to special restrictions and licenses. For example, food-related businesses must follow the guidelines of local and state health departments. The local Environmental Protection Agency grants permits for businesses involved with toxic materials or wastes. Some professional and tradespeople require occupational licenses which are generally issued through the state's Department of Consumer Affairs. These special licenses are for the purpose of protecting the consumer.

Contact the business license bureau in your city or county, as well as local and state agencies with jurisdiction over any occupational licenses. Failure to obtain the necessary licenses or permits can lead to fines and/or business closure.

Once you have determined that your home location can satisfy zoning, legal, and licensing requirements for business, you should analyze the pros and cons of the home office. The following chapter outlines some of the more common reasons for locating a business in the home and illustrates how these initial advantages can turn into disadvantages without careful planning.

ADVANTAGES AND DISADVANTAGES OF THE HOME OFFICE

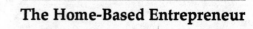

THE HOME-BASED ENTREPRENEUR

ADVANTAGES AND DISADVANTAGES OF THE HOME OFFICE

For some, working at home can be a wonderful experience. For others, it can be a nightmare. Initial advantages can become disadvantages. This chapter is not meant to be discouraging. It is meant to realistically present the advantages and disadvantages of a business based in the home. A home is inherently a private place. A business must be a public entity and therein lies the conflict.

Most entrepreneurs express a need for **independence.** To be able to work on their own with no outside direction is a goal for many. As a home-based entrepreneur, you may be making **all** of the business decisions. There will be no requisitions to central supply when you need a new piece of office equipment or when you run out of typing paper. You will be responsible for evaluating office equipment and making the buying decision. You will also be responsible for ordering supplies. You have the ultimate responsibility for major and minor purchases. The "buck stops with you"! At times, this responsibility can be overwhelming. If you have formed a partnership or corporation, there are other officers to share responsibilities. The sole-proprietor must shoulder these responsibilities or delegate them to family members or employees. The home entrepreneur often overextends himself by trying to do too much.

The home office allows for a **flexibility** in scheduling not practical in an outside office setting. The home entrepreneur sets the schedule for days off and number and time of hours worked per day. Days off can be changed to accommodate one's personal lifestyle. Nights and weekends hours can be used.

Independence and flexibility are two frequently cited advantages which can easily become problems for some. The home entrepreneur must be self-disciplined. "Getting to work" can be interrupted by service calls, deliveries, sick children, television, housework, errands, and personal business. Also, without a "boss" on the premises, it may be difficult to do the least

---

appealing tasks. The home office is not a practical location for a procrastinator! Eventually, most people who work from home find the need for setting up a work schedule. To be effective, one must set limits and plan time. Establish a routine or schedule that works for you and stick to it. Develop good time management skills.

The home office can lead to a feeling of **isolation** from peers and colleagues. The office which served as a source of social contact and friendships is no longer present. The hustle and bustle of a busy office setting will be missed along with the support group of fellow workers. In a home office, zoning restrictions may not allow on-site sales. Often most business is conducted over the phone and face-to-face contact with a client is not possible. This isolation may be further complicated by restrictions on hiring employees to work in an office in a home.

The inherent isolation associated with the home office can be overcome by getting out of the house when you are not working. Keep up your social contacts. Plan meetings outside your home. Join trade and professional associations in order to develop a support group. We all need to be able to share our successes and failures, victories and frustrations with others in our field of business.

We read a lot about **stress** and its effect on our well-being. In an outside office site, we are bombarded by background noise, our eyes are strained by fluorescent lighting, and we are interrupted by the conversations and telephone calls involving other employees. We deal with the expense, lost hours, and noxious fumes encountered when commuting to and from work. The home office sounds like a refuge, a quiet place in which to work, and, with planning, it can be that haven.

One of the pitfalls of the home office is that it can take over the home and the life of the owner. Because you don't "leave" work, the tendency is to work longer hours. The work is always there. If not careful, the home office can become a twenty-four hour a day job and lead to even more stress than encountered in a work setting outside the home office.

If your business is to grow and prosper, you will have little time to spare. Protect your free hours. You must set limits and plan your time. Determine the hours when your office will be open for business. During off hours, use an answering machine. Confine your office area to one room and close the door when office hours are over.

The lack of **child care** facilities and the high cost of day care leads many parents to opt for the home-based business. The flexibility of the work schedule can allow the parent to spend more time with family members. The parent can be at home when children arrive from school. They are available to share the child's school experiences. By scheduling work time, the parent can take part in school and extra-curricular activities. It is felt that the home office can eliminate the need for day care.

While the decision to locate the business in the home is often made in order to spend more time with the children, the discovery is soon made that it is difficult to work productively with small children around. The primary care giver remains the primary care giver and there may be too many demands on the parent's time. Working early morning and late evening hours in order to be free to care for pre-school children may just not be practical. Most parents with a home office resort to locating child care in or outside of the home.

A home-based business can have a tremendous **impact on the family.** There is a loss of privacy as the business spills over into family time. There is a strain placed on family members as they become the primary social contacts as a result of the isolation of the home business. If family members become closely involved in the business, they can be placed in employee/employer roles which put added strain on relationships.

Place as much separation as possible between your working life and home life. Get a separate telephone line for business and use an answering machine when you are not working. Confine your business to one room and close the door when the work day ends. The business should not spill over to the dining table or living room.

Unfortunately, in our society, much of a person's worth is viewed in terms of one's job. The home-based business has an uphill battle in gaining credibility in the marketplace. There seems to be a stigma attached to the home office: it is perceived as an outgrowth of a hobby or as a part-time endeavor. You and your business are in competition with all other businesses which offer your product or service in the marketplace. You only differ in terms of location. It is imperative that you project a **professional image.** Professionalism leads to credibility.

Be proud of your business and take it seriously. Don't let a relaxed home environment make you less disciplined. A clean, organized environment will contribute to your self-esteem and motivation. It will enhance your customer's perception of home-business.

Often **friends and neighbors** must be re-educated as to the realities of home-based business. Inform them that you are serious about your work and will need to be productive during your established working hours. One of the most serious problems faced by the person working in their home is the well-meaning friend or relative who drops by for coffee or a chat because they "know you are home all day". Sometimes this is a difficult problem to solve without hurting the feeling's of a friend or relative, but it is essential to face up to the situation if your working hours are to be spent productively.

There are **financial advantages** to locating a business in the home. Money is saved on parking, lunches, child care, and wardrobe. It is more economical to work at home than to rent or buy office space elsewhere. The home office allows for a gradual business start-up. Outside office space entails additional expenses for utilities, insurance, furnishing, and maintenance. Time and money are saved by eliminating commuting to and from work. Eliminating a 30 minute one-way commute saves 10 hours per week of time.

Home-based business can have a positive effect on the **community.** A reduction in the number of commuters can lead to a corresponding reduction in use of fuel, a decrease in air pollution, and less traffic congestion. On a local level, the neighborhood becomes the center of the home business owner's activities. Near-by businesses such as print shops and office supply stores are patronized. Having someone visible in the area can create more secure neighborhoods through Neighborhood Watch participation. As the owner's focus is more neighborhood-oriented, interest increases in community activities. On a personal basis, the owner gets to know the community and the neighborhood better.

This chapter has presented some of the pros and cons of the home business in order to prepare you for some of the pitfalls inherent in the location. By being forewarned, you can plan ahead for the success of your business. Following are 10 tips for keeping the advantages of home-business for turning to disadvantages:

1. Start the day in a professional manner. Dress appropriately for your work.

2. Establish and observe regular working hours.

3. Establish a routine or schedule that works for you.

4. Make business calls during normally established working hours. Use an answering machine during non-working hours.

5. Maintain a separate room or work area for your office.

6. Treat interruptions as if you were working at a job outside the home.

7. Re-educate family, friends, and neighbors regarding your business and its hours.

8. Get out of the house at least once a day.

9. Keep your contacts with colleagues through trade and professional associations.

10. Protect your free time: no business calls, customers, "shop talk" during non-business hours.

MAINTAIN A SEPARATE ROOM OR WORK AREA FOR YOUR OFFICE.

CLOSE THE DOOR TO YOUR OFFICE WHEN THE WORK-DAY ENDS. PROTECT YOUR FREE HOURS. GOOD LUCK ON THIS ONE !!

A CLEAR, ORGANIZED ENVIRONMENT WILL CONTRIBUTE TO YOUR SELF-ESTEEM AND MOTIVATION.

THE BUSINESS SHOULD NOT "SPILL OVER" TO THE DINING ROOM TABLE OR TO THE LIVING ROOM.

START THE DAY IN A PRO-
FESSIONAL MANNER. DRESS
APPROPRIATELY FOR WORK.

INFORM FRIENDS AND
NEIGHBORS THAT YOU ARE
SERIOUS ABOUT YOUR
WORK AND THAT YOU WILL
HAVE TO BE PRODUCTIVE
DURING ESTABLISHED WORK-
ING HOURS.

THE HOME OFFICE ALLOWS
FOR A GRADUAL BUSINESS
START-UP.

HAVING SOMEONE AT HOME
AND VISIBLE IN YOUR AREA
CAN CREATE MORE SECURE
NEIGHBORHOODS THROUGH
"NEIGHBORHOOD WATCH"
PARTICIPATION.

PERSONAL ASSESSMENT

4 THE HOME-BASED ENTREPRENEUR

PERSONAL ASSESSMENT

Along with examining the advantages and disadvantages of the home office, it is necessary to realistically look at whether or not you have the desire and drive to be self-employed. There are many "tests" available to determine your potential as an entrepreneur. Most are based on the individual's ability to take risks. In fact, one such test gives extra points if you were the first child off the high dive board! These tests would indicate that the more risks you are willing to take, the higher your score, and the better your chances are of being an entrepreneur. Well, entrepreneurs do take risks, but the successful ones don't throw caution to the wind. Taking risks must be tempered with education and good judgement. Perhaps a more practical test for a potential home-based entrepreneur would be to ask some realistic questions about personal traits and business knowledge.

1. Do you enjoy spending time in your home? This seems like an obvious question but one not often faced prior to locating the office in the home. Once the home office is established, business and private time will be spent in the home. If you are not comfortable in your surroundings and the location is not conducive to work, you may find it hard to be productive. Analyze the home setting. Is there adequate space for an office? What is your family situation? How will your customers or clients view your home office?

2. Are you goal-oriented or self-motivated? This is very important because you will be responsible for setting your own work hours, determining your work schedule, and fixing priorities. Entrepreneurship is no job for a procrastinator! You must be able to make decisions.

3. Do you understand financial statements such as cash flow, profit & loss, and balance sheet? These are the tools which can show the financial health of your business. Often, business owners turn their accounts over to someone else because they don't "have time" or "don't want to be bothered". To be

---

successful, the entrepreneur must be willing to learn basic recordkeeping and must be able to interpret the business' financial statements. You, as the business owner, are responsible for determining the financial health of your business through analyzing your financial records.

4. Do you know the resources available to you through the Small Business Administration, your public or college library, and the Chamber of Commerce? The entrepreneur cannot be expected to know everything about business, but he must know where to get the answers to his questions. Good entrepreneurs are not afraid to ask questions.

Obviously, this list of questions is not complete. Entrepreneurs are people who have good self-esteem, a high level of energy, can set and work toward long range goals, and can take the initiative and assume personal responsibility. They enjoy problem solving and take moderate risks. They compete with themselves and learn from failure. How do you rate yourself in these areas?

In the last chapter, we looked at the advantages and disadvantages of the home office. Look, at each one in terms of your own situation. How would you handle the potential pitfalls? In this chapter, you analyzed your personal traits and business knowledge. After taking a good look at your situation, it's time to find a business which suits you. The next chapter looks at skills and interests and presents a list of home-based business possibilities.

HOW TO FIND A BUSINESS

THE HOME-BASED ENTREPRENEUR

HOW TO FIND A BUSINESS

I think it is safe to say that everyone has, at some time in their life, had a dream of owning a business. We all have ideas that come into our minds for new products, adaptions of existing products, or of new ways of providing services. Often, these ideas never quite make it out of our minds and into the marketplace. We are afraid that we don't have the knowledge and skills to create a successful business. Well, the business knowledge will be given to you in later chapters. This chapter will look at ways to find a business which will match your skills and interests.

Perhaps one of the easiest businesses to develop on a home-based level would be to continue your current career on your own. Look at your existing job skills. Could they be developed into an independent business? Good examples would be accounting services, insurance representatives, typists, payroll services, writers, and computer programmers. Any specialized skill or knowledge may be turned into a business.

Look at your hobbies and leisure time activities. Do they lend themselves to a business enterprise? You may provide a service which locates and refinishes antiques. A travel planning service could be developed by someone with a good knowledge of the world and a love of travel. Perhaps you could teach or consult in your area of interest.

Often home equipment can be put to use. Your home computer could be used to provide professional computer-related services. Video recording equipment could be used in a service business which provides video recordings of weddings, business meetings, and other events. Audio taping and duplicating equipment may be used to record seminars and workshops for later duplication and sale.

Listen for problems. Any task or responsibility that people don't like to do for themselves can be developed into a service business. House cleaning, home repair, proof-reading, and gift buying and wrapping are a few services that come to mind.

You may wish to explore a completely new area of interest. Take classes, apprentice, or work part-time in a new area before developing your business. For example, if you are interested in catering, work in a restaurant part-time in order to get your "business education". You will learn about food handling, the health code, invoicing, customer relations, and will be able to see if you really do enjoy working with food. When entering a new area of interest, it is better to keep your current job and moonlight in the new field, if possible, while you determine if you are interested enough in the new area to develop a full-time business. The additional money can be put aside to start your business.

Evaluate current buying trends in order to anticipate new products which will need service. Trade journals and participation in professional associations are excellent resources for keeping ahead of the market. For example, new equipment such as FAX machines and cellular phones will need repair. Why not be the first to offer mobile repair of this equipment?

Try to match your skills and your interests. If you are skilled at writing and are interested in foods, perhaps you could write a dining guide or a restaurant review column for a magazine or newspaper. If you have mechanical skills and are interested in music boxes, a music box repair business could be profitable. Match your skills and interests with the needs of the marketplace. Be flexible. Often your original idea for a product or service will be altered by customer demand. Remember that in order to be successful, you must have a customer who is willing to pay for your product or service. At the same time that you are finding a business, you will be determining a need for that business in the marketplace. The chapter on Market Research will give you the guidelines you will need.

TYPES OF BUSINESSES COMPATIBLE WITH A HOME OFFICE

The following businesses can operate quite successfully when run from the home office. Often, service businesses perform their work at the client's place of business or premises and it is not cost effective to pay rent on another location. This list is by no means complete, but is offered to give you an idea of the variety of types of businesses suited to the home office.

Accounting Services
Advertising Consultant
Animal Care
Answering Service
Antique Refinishing
Appliance Repair
Architect
Artist/Craftsman
Attorney
Audiotaping Service

Baby-sitting
Beautician
Bed and Breakfast Inn
Bee-keeper
Bicycle Mechanic
Billing/Invoicing Service
Bookkeeper
Bridal Consultant

Carpenter
Catalog - drop-shipping
Child Care
Closet Organization
Clothing Alteration
Computer-related Services
Consulting
Courier/Messenger
CPA

Data Processor
Delivery Service
Dentist
Designer
Desktop Publishing
Diet Consultant
Doctor
Drama Coach
Dressmaker
Driving Instruction

Editor
Educational Consultant
Elderly Care Specialist
Electronic Repair
Engineering Consultant
Entertainer
Etiquette Consultant
Event Planning
Export
Exterminator

Fashion Consultant
Financial Planner
Floral Arrangement
Foreign Language Tutor
Freight Forwarding
Fundraising
Furniture Repair

Gardener
Genealogist
General Contractor
Gift Manufacturer
Graphic Designer
Greeting Card Designer

Hairdresser
Handicraft Manufacturer
Home Decorator
Home Economist
Housekeeping Service
House Painter
House Sitter

Image Consultant
Import
Instruction
Insurance Agent
Interior Design
Investment Consultant

Janitorial Service
Jewelry Repair
Job Placement
Journalist

Knife Sharpening

Landscaping
Laundry Service
Lecturer
Legal Transcribing
Light Manufacturing
Literary Agent
Locksmith
Lunch Cart Operator

Mail Order
Management Consultant
Marketing Consultant
Meeting Planner
Messenger Service
Moving Service
Musician

Newsletter
Newspaper Columnist

Office Organization

Painter
Personal Shopping
Pet Care
Photography
Piano Tuner
Plumber
Private Teacher
Proofreading
Publicist
Publishing

Real Estate Agent
Referral Service
Rental Management
Repair Service
Researcher
Reupholsterer
Roofer

Sales Representative
Secretarial Services
Show/Exhibition Planner
Sign Painter
Software Specialist
Speaker's Bureau
Speech Therapist
Stenographer

Tailor
Tax Preparation
Teacher
Telemarketing
Toy Maker
Translator
Travel Agent
Tutorial Service
Typing Service

Upholstery Cleaner
Used Computer Broker

Videotaping Service
Vinyl Repair
Voice Coach

Wallpaper Hanger
Wardrobe Consultant
Watch Repair
Wedding Planner
Window Washing Service
Woodworking
Writer

Yard Service
Yoga Instruction

STEPS TO STARTING A BUSINESS

THE HOME-BASED ENTREPRENEUR

STEPS TO STARTING A BUSINESS

In a previous chapter we dealt with the preliminary research needed to determine that your business can satisfy zoning, legal, and licensing regulations for your home location. We looked at the advantages and disadvantages of the home office. We have also dealt with personal assessment and types of business suited to the home office. Now we will look at the logical step-by-step format for starting a business.

Prior to getting the business license, you must have decided on a business name, legal structure, and location. The business license must be issued before filing the DBA or fictitious name statement. Proof of filing the DBA must be presented to the bank before a business bank account can be set up. Setting up your business by following a logical order can save you much time, money, and stress.

CHOOSE A BUSINESS NAME

The first step in organizing your business is to choose your business name. This is an extremely important decision that must take careful consideration and research. You want to choose a name that you like, that projects a positive image for your company, and that is not currently in use. Before deciding on that name, it would be well to consider the following points.

Try to avoid cute and clever names. Obviously, we don't always practice what we preach! Our publishing company is named **Out of Your Mind...and Into the Marketplace.** While the name works with our market by being memorable, it is often misunderstood by the professional entities in the publishing field. Cute and clever names do not project a business-like image. Many wholesalers will not view the business as legitimate even though you may be running a full-scale operation. For example, **Sunshine Art Products** manufactures stained glass gift ware. This home-based company does not have difficulty purchasing stained glass materials wholesale because the name sounds business-like. By contrast, **Kathy's Kute Kritters** manufactures stained glass window hangings featuring animals. Because of the cutesy nature of the name, Kathy, at times, has had difficulty in dealing with major stained glass suppliers who feel that the business sounds like a hobby. Of course, there are exceptions to every rule. Twelve years ago, a group of twenty prospective business owners met for a Small Business Administration seminar in Oakland, CA. The only business name this author remembers from the entire group is **Franks for the Memory,** a cafe featuring hot dogs! The name is memorable. You must make a value judgement based on your business name's perception by your customers and suppliers.

Make your name descriptive to advertise your product or service. The consumer who sees your name should be able to associate it with the product or service you provide. For example, **Brigg's Accounting Services** lets us know what service is being provided. **Briggs and Associates** does not. Often, we collect business cards at meetings and conventions. Later, when we look through the cards, we haven't a clue as to the nature of the business if the name is not descriptive. At the same time, try not to have the name restrictive. You may start by providing one service and later wish to expand into providing auxiliary services or related products. For example, **Kathy's Kute Kritters** indicates that some kind of animal-like product is being crafted. If Kathy chooses to include other stained glass designs, the name will not reflect the new product line. **Kathy's Stained Glass Creations** might have been a better choice. It is not always easy to anticipate the directions your company may take, but try to project your future growth. It is difficult to change your business name once established. You risk losing customers and the good will you have built.

Try to keep your name short and pronounceable. Complicated names are harder to remember. Also, long names will not fit on computer generated mailing labels. Often our mail comes to **Out of Your Mind** because the name is so long. Obviously, this shortening of our name does not add to our credibility!

Consider alphabetical listings in directories. It is to your advantage to be closer to the A's than to the Z's. You have a captive audience through your directory listings. Consumers and clients do not look through business and professional directories unless they are trying to locate products or services. They generally look through the first few listings when deciding who to call.

There may be some advantages to using your own name as part of your business name. If you are already well-respected in your community or field of business, this may be to your advantage. It may give you a head start in the business world. If you use your full legal name, you may not have to file a DBA ("doing business as", which is covered later in this section). If you have a common name, you may still wish to file the DBA for protection of the name in reference to your business. For example, if your name were Tom Adams, you might register **Tom Adams Contracting** because Tom Adams is a common name.

It is very important to check the availability of the business name you have chosen. To the best of your ability, you must determine that the name is not already in use. Check through the phone directories at your public library.

The reference librarian can guide you to the Trademark Directories which will list names which have been trademarked. Check with your city and/ or county business license bureaus for listings of existing businesses. Each state has an office responsible for the registration of names of businesses incorporated within that state, out-of-state corporations qualified to do business in the state, and names which have been registered or reserved by other corporations. Generally, this office falls under the jurisdiction of the Secretary of State. Even if you are not considering forming a corporation as your legal structure, it is to your advantage to use this resource in researching your name availability. If you choose to incorporate later, you will want to use your current name as your corporate name since it will be associated with your product or service. Generally, there is not much problem with name infringement unless you become visible in the marketplace and create a threat to the business which feels it has prior claim to the name. The time you spend in researching name availability can end up being very cost-effective.

Choosing a business name is a very personal decision and not one to be rushed into. Take time to choose a name with which you will be comfortable, which will project your desired company image, and which is available. From the time you begin advertising your business, its name will be in the public eye. Select it with care and it will serve you well.

CHOOSE YOUR LEGAL STRUCTURE

Your next decision will be the choice of a legal structure which best suits your needs and the needs of your particular business. There are three principal kinds of business structures: the sole proprietorship, partnership, and the corporation. The advantages and disadvantages of each structure should be examined in terms of your specific circumstances.

The **sole proprietorship** is owned and operated by one person. This is the simplest, and least expensive business structure to form. Many start-up companies choose this form until it becomes practical to enter into a partnership or to incorporate. One of the advantages of the sole-proprietorship is the ease of formation. There are fewer legal restrictions and it is the least expensive to form. The costs vary according to the city in which the business is formed, but usually include a license fee and may include a business tax. As the sole owner, all profits go to you, as do the losses! You will be taxed as an individual. Your business profit and loss is recorded on Federal Tax Form 1040, Schedule C, and the bottom line amount transferred to your personal tax form. You will also file Schedule SE which is your contribution to Social Security. The control and decision making are vested in you as the owner.

One of the major disadvantages of the sole proprietorship is unlimited personal liability. You will be responsible for the full amount of business debt which may exceed your investment. This liability may extend to personal assets such as home and vehicles. Since financing comes from the proprietor and loans are based on the financial strength of the individual, obtaining long term business financing may be difficult. The future of the company is dependent upon the owner's capabilities in terms of knowledge, drive, and financial potential which may limit growth potential. As the only person responsible for the business, the sole proprietor assumes heavy responsibility.

A **partnership** is a legal business relationship in which two or more people agree to share ownership and management of a business. Often partners are chosen who possesses skills or expertise which are complementary. Sharing ownership of a business may be a way of raising additional capital. Care should be taken when choosing a partner; you will be bound by each other's decisions. Choose carefully based on compatibility of work styles, business practices, character, financial situation, skills, and expertise.

The advantages of a partnership include the ease of formation, the sharing of responsibility, and the increased growth potential. By sharing in the profits, the partners are motivated to succeed. This form allows for the distribution of the work load and allows for a sharing of ideas, skills, and responsibilities. A partnership makes it possible to obtain more capital and to tap into more skills giving the business increased potential.

One of the disadvantages of a partnership is the unlimited personal liability as partners personally are responsible for business debt. While the opportunity for getting long-term financing is greater in a partnership, it is still dependent upon review of the individual partner's assets.

Do not underestimate the need for a partnership agreement. Many friendships and good working relationships have ended over business disputes. Like a sole proprietorship, a partnership terminates as a legal entity upon the death or withdrawal of a general partner unless the partnership agreement provides otherwise. The buying out of a partnership or sale to another party must be spelled out in the agreement. This is also where the terms of profit distribution are stated. Take time and carefully prepare a partnership agreement and have it notarized. It will serve as the guideline for your working relationship with your partners. It will outline the financial, managerial, and material contributions by the partners into the business and delineate the roles of the partners is the business relationship.

The **corporation** is the most complex of the three business structures. A corporation becomes a distinct legal entity separate from the individuals who own it. It is formed by the authority of the State Government with the approval of the Secretary of State. If business is conducted in more than one state, the Federal laws regarding interstate commerce must be observed. Federal and State laws may vary considerably and corporations differ so much in size and type that it is hard to generalize.

The Home-Based Entrepreneur

However, there are several advantages that are common to most corporations. Ownership is readily transferrable and the corporation does not cease to exist with the death of an owner. A corporation has access to numerous investors and can raise substantial capital through the sale of stock. As a separate legal entity, the corporation is responsible and liable for all debt. The shareholders are liable only for the amount they have invested. Authority can be delegated and the corporation has the ability to draw on the expertise and skills of more than one individual.

Extensive government regulations and burdensome local, state, and federal reports can prove to be a disadvantage. A corporation is also expensive to form. Income tax is paid on corporate net income (profit) and on individual salaries and dividends. This double taxation may be avoided in specific instances by electing to form an S corporation.

An **S corporation** allows the small business corporation to have its income taxed to the shareholders as if the corporation were a partnership. One objective is to overcome the double tax feature of taxing corporate income and stockholder dividends separately. There are specific conditions for qualifying for S corporation status. To qualify, a corporation must meet all of the five following requirements.

1. It must be a domestic (United States) corporation.

2. It must have no more than 35 shareholders.

3. None of the shareholders can be non-resident aliens.

4. It must have only one class of stock.

5. All shareholders must be individuals, estates, or certain trusts.

Because of the complexity of the corporation, you may wish to consult an attorney regarding its formation.

The preceding information was presented to help you make a knowledgeable decision regarding the legal structure of your business. You may start as a sole proprietor and later form a partnership as your needs change. You may decide that your needs are better served by starting as a corporation. If you change the structure of an existing business, you must notify the appropriate government entities and file the forms needed to effect the change. A reference list at the end of this book provides a listing of materials which will give you additional information on legal structure. Consult an attorney if you need help in determining the best type of structure for your business.

OBTAIN A BUSINESS LICENSE.

Once you have met with the zoning and business license departments and determined that your business meets all the specific requirements for operation as a home-based business, you are ready to officially apply for the license. Business licenses are generally issued through the City or County Clerk's office and requires completion of an application form. The most common information asked will cover business name, type of legal structure, location, type of business, number of employees, expected gross income, and vehicles to be operated. Upon submission of the application and fee, the application will be reviewed prior to being issued. The license is renewed annually, subject to adherence to the city's codes and regulations.

FILE YOUR DBA

If you plan to conduct your business under a fictitious name, you must file a DBA which stands for **Doing Business As.** It may also be referred to as the **Fictitious Name Statement.** A fictitious name is any business name that does not contain your full legal name as a part of it. In some states, you will be required to file a DBA even if you are using your legal name.

The purpose of the DBA is to inform the general public that you are beginning an operation under an assumed or fictitious name and that you are the individual who will be conducting that business. It must be published in a general circulation newspaper in the **county** in which your business is located. The ad generally must run in 4 consecutive issues. During this time, anyone may challenge your right to do business under that name. Following publication, verification must be filed with the City or County clerk.

Newspaper charges vary for this service and may range from $25.00 to over $150.00 depending upon the size of the newspaper circulation. It pays to shop competitively. Some papers also file the form with the clerk which may save you some additional time. Often, this is worth a small additional fee.

As with the business license, the DBA is renewable. Renewing a DBA does not require republishing, but usually requires a fee. It is your responsibility to keep track of renewal dates.

The DBA gives you the exclusive right to use the name, and keeps others from using the same or similar name. The time and money spent is very small compared to the benefits you will derive from becoming the owner of your business name.

OBTAIN A SELLER'S PERMIT

A **seller's permit number** is required of anyone who purchases items for resale or who provides a taxable service. An example of a taxable service would be clock repair: the labor or repair is not taxable, but the parts may be. This number or permit is required in all states where sales tax is collected. A seller's permit is obtained through the state agency responsible for the collection of sales tax. Most often, it will be the Department of Revenue.

The retailer or final seller, not the customer, is responsible for paying the sales tax. Consequently, every seller engaged in the business of selling a tangible product or of providing a taxable service in a state where sales tax is collected is required to hold a seller's permit for the purpose of reporting and paying their sales and use tax liability. The seller's permit may also be referred to as a **resale number** or a **resale certificate.**

Your application must be based on the fact that you will be purchasing taxable items that you will offer for sale to the ultimate consumer, to other resalers, or that you will be providing a taxable service. Any other reason for your request may be grounds for denial.

In the past, there has been widespread misuse of resale tax numbers. Once you have been issued a number, it is imperative that you use it only for the purpose for which it was intended. The penalties for misuse are very serious and may involve a heavy fine and/or a jail sentence. Misuse has occurred when non-business or personal items have been purchased in order to avoid payment of sales tax. The rule of thumb is: If you do not intend to resell your purchase through your business, do not use your resale number to buy it tax free.

Contact the agency responsible for the collection of sales tax in your state in order to determine the regulations on your particular type of business.

SET UP A BUSINESS BANK ACCOUNT

Often a business owner is tempted to run business finances through personal accounts. It is imperative that you keep your personal and business finances separate. Failure to do so can cause problems with your recordkeeping and tax computations. Business accounts are necessary for credibility when dealing with other businesses. You will not have much credibility with wholesalers or suppliers if you do not pay with a business check.

The first account opened with a bank is usually the business checking account. You must show proof of DBA filing before the account can be opened under your business name. The DBA gives verification that you are authorized to deposit checks made out to the business name. Be sure to take your verification with you. The bank will make a copy for their records.

When you open your account, request that your checks be numbered beginning with a number other than 101. This is a tip-off that you are a new business. You want to look established in the eyes of your creditors.

The selection of the bank with which you will do business should be undertaken with consideration. Banks vary greatly in the services they offer, as well as in the charges for those services. The following are some questions to ask when shopping for a bank

1. Does the bank pay interest on a business checking account?

2. What is the current interest rate?

3. Does the account have a service and/or check charge?

4. What is the charge for returned checks?

5. Does the bank have a holding period on deposits?

6. Does the bank issue a check guarantee card?

7. Does the bank offer a major credit card service?

8. What are the bank's hours of operation?

9. Does the bank have other branches?

10. What other services does the bank offer?

11. Is the bank in a convenient and safe location?

Compare the advantages and disadvantages of the financial institutions being considered. It is important to establish a good working rapport with the bank management and personnel. Perhaps the best question to ask yourself is: What is my overall feeling about this bank? Choose one in which you feel comfortable, which offers the services you need, and that is convenient to your location.

SUCCESS OR FAILURE:
IT DEPENDS ON
YOUR CASH FLOW

THE HOME-BASED ENTREPRENEUR

SUCCESS OR FAILURE:
IT DEPENDS ON YOUR CASH FLOW

It is a known fact that a third or more of today's businesses fail due to a lack of cash flow. What is cash flow? How do you plan ahead to insure your chances of success? The purpose of this chapter will be to introduce you to the concept of "cash flow" and to show you how careful planning can help you to avoid business disaster.

WHAT IS A CASH FLOW STATEMENT?

A cash flow statement is the same as a budget. It is a pro forma (or projected) statement that estimates how much money will flow out of and into a business during a designated period of time, usually the coming tax year. Expenses are paid from cash on hand, sale of assets, revenues from sales and services, money borrowed from a lender, or investments made in exchange for equity in the company. These funds must be used to support the running of the business, repayment of loans and interest, and any personal financial needs of the owners. If your business will require $100,000 to pay its expenses and $50,000 to support the owners, you will need an equal amount of money flowing into the business just to remain at a status quo. Anything less may eventually lead to an inability to pay your creditors--or yourself.

I personally like the term **cash flow**, rather than budget. *Webster's New World Dictionary* defines budget as "a plan or schedule adjusting expenses during a certain period to the estimated or fixed income of that period". This certainly indicates that the planning of a budget requires the estimating of **how much** money we will need in a given amount of time. The same dictionary defines cash flow as "the pattern of receipts and expenditures of a company, government, etc., resulting in the availability or nonavailability of cash". This availability or nonavailability of cash **when** it is needed for expenditures gets to the very heart of the matter. By careful planning, you must try to project not only **how much** cash will have to flow into and out of your business, but also **when** it will need to flow in and out. A business may be able to plan for gross receipts that will cover its needs. However, if those sales do not take place in time to pay the expenses, the business will

---

be past history before the revenues are realized. The publishing industry is a good example of a business that has heavy cash demands as much as six to nine months before it realizes any revenues as a result of those expenditures. If a publisher cannot pay the printer, there will be no books for sale. That printer will not produce your finished product on a promise that he will be paid six to nine months later on a completion of sale and receipt of invoice payment. To keep the business going, the publisher must plan ahead for sources of cash to tide the business over until the revenues are received.

PRE-PLANNING WORKSHEETS

The first step in planning a cash flow statement can be accomplished by preparing two worksheets:

1. **CASH TO BE PAID OUT (CASH FLOWING OUT OF YOUR BUSINESS)**

2. **SOURCES OF CASH (CASH FLOWING INTO YOUR BUSINESS)**

CASH TO BE PAID OUT

The Cash to be Paid Out (Cash Flowing Out of Your Business) Worksheet is used to estimate how much cash will be expended by your business in the coming year. You may wish to approach the task by compiling several individual budgets, such as: cost of goods, direct expenses, administrative expenses, owner draws, etc. These expenditures are not always easy to estimate. If you are a new business, it will be necessary for you to do lots of market research. If you are an existing business, you will combine information from the past financial statements with trends in your particular industry.

SOURCES OF CASH

The Sources of Cash (Cash Flowing Into Your Business) Worksheet is used to estimate how much cash will be available from what sources. To complete this worksheet, you will have to look at cash on hand, projected revenues, assets that can be liquidated, possible lenders or investors, and owner equity to be contributed. This worksheet will force you to take a look at any existing possibilities for increasing available cash.

On the pages that follow, you will find examples of the two worksheets along with accompanying information explaining each of the categories used. The worksheets are filled in for a fictitious company, **ABC PUBLISHING CO.** Please note that the Cash to be Paid Out Worksheet shows a need for

$131,000. It was necessary in projecting Sources of Cash to account for $131,000 without the projected sales because their receipt is expected to take place at the end of the year in question. Next year, those revenues would be reflected in cash on hand or other saleable assets. Be sure to figure all estimates on both worksheets for the same period of time (annually, quarterly, monthly, etc.)

EXPLANATION OF CATEGORIES
CASH TO BE PAID OUT WORKSHEET

1. START-UP COSTS

These are the costs incurred by you to get your business underway. They usually are a one-time expense and are capitalized for tax purposes.

2. INVENTORY PURCHASES

Cash to be spent during the period on items intended for resale. If you purchase manufactured products, this includes the cash outlay for those purchases.

If you are the manufacturer, include labor and materials on units to be produced.

3. SELLING EXPENSE (Direct Expense)

These are the costs of all expenses that will relate directly to your product or service (other than manufacturing costs or purchase price of inventory).

4. OPERATING EXPENSE (Indirect Expense)

Include all expected costs of office overhead. If certain bills must be paid ahead, include total cash outlay even if covered period extends into the next year.

5. ASSETS (Long-Term Purchases)

These are the capital assets that will be depreciated over a period of years. Determine how you intend to pay for them and include all cash to be paid out in the current period.

6. LIABILITIES

What are the payments you expect to have to make to retire any debts or loans? Do you have any Accounts Payable as you begin the new year? You will need to determine the amount of cash outlay that will need to be paid in the current year. If you have a car loan for $20,000 and you pay $500 per month, you will have a cash outlay of $6,000 for the coming year.

7. OWNER EQUITY

This item is frequently overlooked in planning cash flow. If you, as the business owner, will need a draw of $2,000 per month to live on, you must plan for $24,000 cash flowing out of your business in the coming year. Even though this is not a deductible expense for your business, failure to plan for it may cause your business to go under.

ABC PUBLISHING CO.

CASH TO BE PAID OUT WORKSHEET

(CASH FLOWING OUT OF YOUR BUSINESS)

START-UP COSTS:

Business License (annual expense)	$ 30.00
DBA Filing Fee (one-time cost)	50.00
Other start-up costs:	920.00
_____	____
_____	____
_____	____

INVENTORY PURCHASES — 35,000.00
Cash out for items for resale or services

SELLING EXPENSE (DIRECT EXPENSE)

Advertising	$10,000
Freight	3,500
Packaging Costs	500
Parts & Supplies	—
Sales Salaries	15,000
Misc. Direct Exp.	2,000
TOTAL DIRECT EXPENSE	31,000.00

OPERATING EXPENSE (INDIRECT EXPENSE)

Insurance	1,000
Licenses & Permits	100
Office Salaries	18,000
Rent Expense	—
Utilities	3,000
Misc. Indirect Exp.	2,000
TOTAL INDIRECT EXPENSE	24,100.00

ASSETS (LONG-TERM PURCHASES) — 6,000.00
Cash to be paid out in current period

LIABILITIES — 9,900.00
Cash outlay for retiring debts, loans,
and/or accounts payable

OWNER EQUITY — 24,000.00
Cash to be withdrawn by owner

TOTAL CASH TO BE PAID OUT............. $ 131,000.00

Note: Be sure to use the same time period throughout your worksheets monthly,
quarterly, annually.

EXPLANATION OF CATEGORIES
SOURCES OF CASH WORKSHEET

1. CASH ON HAND

Money you have on hand. Be sure to include petty cash and monies not yet deposited.

2. SALES · REVENUES

This will include all of the expected revenues from the sale of your product or service. If payment is not expected during the time period covered by this worksheet, do not include that portion of your sales. Do include deposits you require on expected sales or services. When figuring collections on Accounts Receivable, you will have to project the percentage of invoices that will be lost to bad debts and subtract it from your Accounts Receivable total.

3. MISCELLANEOUS INCOME

Do you, or will you have, any monies out on loan or depositedin accounts that will yield interest income during the period in question?

4. SALE OF LONG-TERM ASSETS

If you are expecting to sell any of your fixed assets such asland, buildings, vehicles, machinery, equipment, etc., be sure to include only the cash you will receive on those sales during the current period.

5. LIABILITIES

This figure represents the amount you will be able to borrow from lending institutions such as banks, finance companies, the S.B.A., etc. Be reasonable about what you think you can borrow. If you have no collateral, have no business plan, and you have a poor financial history, you will find it difficult if not impossible to find a lender. This source of cash requires lots of pre-planning and perseverance.

6. EQUITY

Sources of equity come from owner investments, contributed capital, sale of stock, or venture capital. Do you anticipate the availability of personal funds? Does your business have the potential for growth that might interest a venture capitalist? Be sure to be realistic in this area, also. You cannot sell stock (or equity) to a nonexistent investor.

ABC PUBLISHING CO.

SOURCES OF CASH WORKSHEET
(CASH FLOWING INTO YOUR BUSINESS)

1. CASH ON HAND — $ 20,000

2. SALES-REVENUES

Sales — NOTE: WILL NOT BE RECEIVED UNTIL November & December — (90,000)
Service Income — 24,000
Deposits on Sales or Services — 0
Collections on Accounts Receivable — 0

3. MISCELLANEOUS INCOME

Interest Income — 1,000

4. SALE OF LONG-TERM ASSETS — 0

5. LIABILITIES

Loans (Banks, Finance Cos., S.B.A., etc.) — 40,000

6. EQUITY

Owner Investments (Sole Prop. or Partnership) — 10,000 (C.D.)
Contributed Capital (Corporation) —
Sale of Stock (Corporation) —
Venture Capital — 35,000

TOTAL CASH AVAILABLE — $ 131,000 – WITHOUT SALES

$ 221,000 – WITH SALES

BUILDING THE CASH FLOW STATEMENT

Now that you have completed the two worksheets, you are ready to use that information to build your ProForma Cash Flow Statement. You have estimated **how much** cash will be needed for the year and you now know the sources that are available. In this phase of cash flow planning you will break the time period of one year into monthly segments and predict **when** the cash will be needed to make the financial year flow smoothly. To make the job easier, you can follow these steps:

1. Figure the cost-of-goods, direct and indirect expenses out in monthly increments. Most will vary. When do you plan to purchase the most inventory? What months will require the most advertising? Are you expecting a rent or insurance increase? When will commissions be due on expected sales?

2. Project your sales on a monthly basis. Be sure their projections are based on payment of invoices. There will be no cash flowing in on unpaid invoices. If your income is from services, project your revenues according to demand for your particular service and how readily you can fill that demand. If you do not have employees other than yourself, remember that income ceases when you are on vacation.

3. Determine what you will need in the way of long-term assets. When will you need them? How much will the payments be and when will they begin?

4. Fill in as much of the cash flow statement as you can using the preceding projections and any others you can comfortably determine. Then proceed according to the directions for completing the rest.

To clarify the process of filling in a proforma cash flow statement, the next two pages have been devoted to walking you through January and part of February for ABC Publishing Company. The last two pages of the chapter contain the Directions for Completing a ProForma Cash Flow Statement and a Form for your use in your own projections.

SUMMARY

The ProForma Cash Flow Statement is one of the most useful tools in Business Planning. It is one of the first financial projections to be examined by a potential lender. Be realistic about your projections. At the close of each business month compare your ProForma Cash Flow Statement with your Profit and Loss Statement and revise future projections accordingly. You will find that the proper attention paid to this process will be very beneficial in helping you to implement changes that will make your business more profitable.

Good Luck! Even the authors realize that this is a formidable task. Grit your teeth and dig in. You can do it!

ABC PUBLISHING CO.
JAN-FEB 1990

JANUARY PROJECTIONS

1. ABC projects a beginning cash balance of $20,000.00.

2. Cash Receipts-Books have not yet been published, so there will be no sales. However, a teaching income of $4,000.00 is projected.

3. Interest on the $20,000.00 will amount to about $100.00 at current rates.

4. There are no Long-Term assets to sell.

5. Adding 1,2,3 & 4 the Total Cash Available will be $24,100.00.

6. Cash Payments-Books will not be published in Feb. and no cash will be required by the printer in January. However, there will be desktop publishing and graphics costs of $5,000.00.

7. Direct Expenses-Estimated at $1,140.00.

8. Indirect Expenses-Estimated at $815.00.

9. Interest Expense-No outstanding debts or loans-no interest.

10. Taxes-No profit has been made-no estimated taxes due.

11. Payments on Long-Term Assets-Plan to purchase office equipment to be paid in full at time of purchase $1139.00.

12. Loan Repayments-No loans have been made.

13. Owner Draws-Owner will need $2,000.00 for living expenses.

14. Total Cash Paid Out-Add 6 through 13. Total $10,494.00.

15. Cash Balance-Subtract Cash Paid Out from Total Cash Available. The result is $13,606.00.

16. Loans to be Received-Being aware of the $30,000.00 printer's charge for February, a loan of $40,000.00 has been anticipated to increase Cash Available. (This requires advance planning!!)

17. Equity Deposit-Owner plans to add $5,000.00 from a personal account.

18. Ending Cash Balance-Adding 15,16, & 17 the result is $58,606.00.

FEBRUARY PROJECTIONS

1. Beginning Cash Balance-January's Ending Cash Balance is transferred to February's Beginning Balance — $58,606.00.

2. Cash Receipts-Still no sales, but teaching income of $2,000.00.

3. Interest Income-is projected at about $120.00.

4. Sale of Long-Term Assets-NONE.

5. Total Cash Available-Add 1,2,3 & 4. The result $60,726.00.

6. Cash Payments — $30,000.00 book printing charge and $400.00 graphics.

ABC PUBLISHING CO.

	JAN	FEB
BEG. CASH BALANCE	$20,000	$58,606
CASH RECEIPTS		
a. Sales.Revenues	4,000	2,000
b. Interest Income	100	120
c. Sale of Long-Term Assets		
TOTAL CASH AVAILABLE	24,100	60,726
CASH PAYMENTS		
a. COST OF GOODS TO BE SOLD		
1. Purchases		30,000
2. Material		
3. Labor	5,000	400
b. DIRECT EXPENSES		
1. Advertising	300	
2. Freight	120	
3. Packaging Costs		
4. Parts & Supplies	270	
5. Salaries		
6. Misc. Dir. Exp.	450	
c. INDIRECT EXPENSES		
1. Insurance	80	
2. Licenses & Permits	125	
3. Office Salaries	200	
4. Rent Expenses	500	
5. Utilities	110	
6. Misc. Indir. Exp.	200	
7.		
d. INTEREST EXPENSE		
e. FEDERAL INCOME TAX		
f. OTHER TAXES		
g. PAYTS ON L-TERM ASSETS	1,139	
h. LOAN REPAYMENTS		
i. OWNER DRAWS	2,000	
TOTAL CASH PAID OUT	10,494	
CASH BALANCE/DEFICIENCY	13,606	
LOANS TO BE RECEIVED	40,000	
EQUITY DEPOSITS	5,000	
ENDING CASH BALANCE	$58,606	

(FEB column: CONT. as in JAN.)

DIRECTIONS FOR COMPLETING YOUR
PRO FORMA CASH FLOW STATEMENT

NOTE:
1. Horizontal Columns are divided into the twelve months and preceded by a "Total Column."

2. Vertical positions of the statement contain all the sources of the cash and cash to be paid out. These figures are retrieved from the two previous worksheets and from Individual Budgets.

The figures are projected for each month reflecting the flow of cash in and out of your business for a one-year period. Begin with January and proceed as follows:

1. Project the Beginning Cash Balance. Enter that figure under the heading "January".

2. Project Cash Receipts for January.

3. Add the Beginning Cash Balance and the Cash Receipts to determine the Cash Available.

4. Project the Expenses, Taxes, Loan Repayments and Draws to be made in January.

5. Total the Expenses to determine Total Cash Paid Out.

6. Subtract Cash Paid Out from Total Cash Available.

7. If the result of No. 6 is negative, enter under Cash Deficiency.

8. Anticipate any Loans to be Received and enter.

9. Add anticipated loans to cash remaining after expenses (or Cash Deficiency) to project the Ending Cash Balance for January.

10. The Ending Cash Balance for January is carried to February and becomes the February Beginning Cash Balance.

11. The process is repeated until December is completed.

To Complete "TOTAL COLUMN":

1. The Beginning Cash Balance for January is entered in the first space of the "Total Column."

2. The monthly figures for each category are added horizontally and the result entered in the corresponding category under Total.

3. The Total Column is computed in the same manner as the individual months. If you have been accurate in your computation, the December Ending Cash Balance will be exactly the same as the Total Ending Cash Balance.

This process may seem complicated, but as you work with it, I think it will begin to make perfect sense and will be a straight-forward and reasonable task to accomplish.

PRO FORMA CASH FLOW STATEMENT

FOR THE YEAR 19 ____

	TOTAL	JAN	FEB	MAR	APR	MAY	JUN	JUL	AUG	SEP	OCT	NOV	DEC
BEG. CASH BALANCE													
CASH RECEIPTS													
a. Sales.Revenues													
b. Interest Income													
c. Sale of Long-Term Assets													
TOTAL CASH AVAILABLE													
CASH PAYMENTS													
a. COST OF GOODS TO BE SOLD													
1. Purchases													
2. Material													
3. Labor													
b. DIRECT EXPENSES													
1. Advertising													
2. Freight													
3. Packaging Costs													
4. Parts & Supplies													
5. Salaries													
6. Misc. Dir. Exp.													
c. INDIRECT EXPENSES													
1. Insurance													
2. Licenses & Permits													
3. Office Salaries													
4. Rent Expenses													
5. Utilities													
6. Misc. Indir. Exp.													
7.													
d. INTEREST EXPENSE													
e. FEDERAL INCOME TAX													
f. OTHER TAXES													
g. PAYTS ON L-TERM ASSETS													
h. LOAN REPAYMENTS													
i. OWNER DRAWS													
TOTAL CASH PAID OUT													
CASH BALANCE/DEFICIENCY													
LOANS TO BE RECEIVED													
EQUITY DEPOSITS													
ENDING CASH BALANCE													

RECORDKEEPING FOR A HOME-BASED BUSINESS

THE HOME-BASED ENTREPRENEUR

RECORDKEEPING FOR A HOME-BASED BUSINESS

THE IMPORTANCE OF RECORDKEEPING

Recordkeeping has two main functions:

1. To provide you with tax information that can be easily retrieved and verified.

2. To provide you with information that will help you to see trends and implement changes during the life of your business.

To be the most effective you should set up a system that is as simple as possible and yet complete enough to give you any information that will be helpful in your business. If you have a personal computer, you may be able to utilize it in your record keeping, but only if you have a good working knowledge of both recordkeeping and the operation of the computer. Don't look for an easy way out by thinking that you can run to the computer store, buy a program, plug it in, and solve all of your problems. Every business is different and therefore will have its own individual accounting needs.

SHOULD YOU HIRE AN ACCOUNTANT?

Whether or not you hire an accountant, it is advisable that you learn the basics of small business accounting. If your funds are limited, you can learn to do everything but your tax returns. There are textbooks and courses available that will enable you to keep a very adequate set of records. It is our opinion that you should use an accountant at year end to maximize your tax benefits. There are very few of us who are knowledgeable about all of the fine points and changes in tax laws. If you establish a good relationship with an accountant, he or she can also help you with questions that arise during the year.

If you are financially able and feel more comfortable in having an accountant do all of your bookkeeping, you will still be wise to educate yourself about the basics. Ask him/her to prepare a Balance Statement and a Profit & Loss Statement at the close of every month and be secure in the knowledge that you will be able to read and understand them. The information is essential to the effective running of your business.

WHEN DO YOU BEGIN?

If you are reading this book, you are thinking about or have already gone into business. So now is the time to begin keeping records. If you are successful and get your doors open, all of the expenses you incurred in start-up will be valid costs of doing business. Failure to record them will invalidate them as deductible expenses at tax time.

You can start by keeping a journal of your daily activities--where you went, who you saw, what it cost you. Keep track of entrepreneurial classes, mileage, supplies purchased, telephone calls,professional materials, and anything else that might relate to your business venture. If your idea does not turn into an active business, the only thing you will have lost is a little bit of time.

DO YOU NEED TO SEPARATE BUSINESS AND PERSONAL FINANCES?

One of the most common mistakes made by small-business owner's--and especially home-based business owner's--is that of mixing business and personal finances. We often get asked in recordkeeping classes if it is necessary to open a separate business bank account. The answer is "Yes". You should never mix business and personal monies. It is next to impossible to keep them sorted out without a separate bank account. Not only does the IRS require a strict accounting of business finances, but good business practices demand it. Slipshod methods of recordkeeping will only lead to a decrease in your profits and heartaches at tax times.

ARE THE RECORDS DIFFERENT FOR A HOME-BASED BUSINESS?

In general, recordkeeping for a home-based business is exactly the same as for any other business. There are some IRS restrictions as to what is necessary in order for your home to qualify as a business expense. There are also guidelines as to how to figure percentages of those expenses that benefit both your home and your business. The chapter entitled **TAX DEDUCTIONS FOR A HOME-BASED BUSINESS** will answer many of your questions. For more detailed information, you can study the **free** IRS publication 587, "Business Use of Your Home".

WHAT SUPPLIES ARE NEEDED FOR BASIC BUSINESS RECORDKEEPING?

New business owners frequently go to a local stationary store and find themselves in a quandary as to what to purchase in the way of bookkeeping supplies. To save you time, the following is a checklist of items that will probably come in handy regardless of your type of business. We have included both recordkeeping and general office supplies.

1. Files

    a. Two drawer filing cabinet
    b. Large A-Z accordian file
    c. Divided file folders

2. Yearly Books

    a. 12-column ledger (General Journal)
    b. Bound Journal (Petty Cash, Travel, etc.)
    c. Inventory Record

3. General Office Supplies

    a. Pens and pencils (red and black)
    b. Tape dispenser and tape
    c. Stapler and staples
    d. 12 inch ruler
    e. Scissors

4. Business Forms

    a. Letterhead and envelopes
    b. Invoices
    c. Resale Certificates

5. Packaging Supplies

    a. Packaging tape
    b. Mailing labels
    c. Return address stamp

If you find a good office supply store that carries most of the items you use, you may wish to open a commercial account with them. They often have other services which you can utilize as well, such as copy and printing services. Having an open account will generally give you about a 10% discount on your purchases.

WHAT RECORDS DO YOU NEED TO KEEP?

It is not the purpose of this book to give you a course in small-business accounting. However, we will attempt in the next few pages to acquaint you with the basic records that you will need to keep. For more detailed information, we have written a book entitled **Recordkeeping: The Secret to Growth & Profit.** There are also many fine accounting books available in the public libraries. Classes can be taken through most Community Colleges and the IRS gives small business tax classes at various locations on a regular basis.

GENERAL RECORDS

Every business will require certain records to keep track of its activities during the tax year. The most common are as follows:

1. General Journal

2. Petty Cash Record

3. Inventory Records

4. Fixed Assets Log

5. Accounts Payable

6. Accounts Receivable

7. Travel and Entertainment Records

8. Customer Records

9. Business Checkbook

These records will contain the information that will be used to develop your monthly financial statements--the Balance Sheet and Profit & Loss Statement. It is necessary for you to set up a General Recordkeeping Schedule and keep your records current on a regular basis--the frequency depending upon the your volume of business. To acquaint you with these records, we will define each one and include sample forms at the back of the chapter.

1. **General Journal** — a columnar book used to record transactions made by your business. The transactions are recorded as revenues and expenses. The revenues are all transactions for which monies are received. The expenses are all transactions for which monies are paid out.

2. **Petty Cash Record** — petty cash refers to all the purchases made with cash or personal checks when it is not convenient to pay with a business check. They are recorded in a separate journal and paid

by periodically writing a business check that is recorded as an expense in the General Journal and a deposit in the Petty Cash Record. Petty Cash transactions require careful recording.

3. **Inventory Records** — these are records that keep track of all items purchased or manufactured for resale. The IRS requires a beginning and ending inventory each year. Inventory control is a major factor in business success. Internal use of these records will greatly enhance your profits.

4. **Fixed Assets Log** — This is a list of all assets that will have to be capitalized. These are items purchased for use in your business at a cost of $100.00 or more and not debited to an expense account. They are depreciated over a period of more than one year. Examples might be as follows: vehicles, office equipment, production equipment, buildings, etc.

5. **Accounts Payable** — a record of debts owed by your company for goods purchased or services rendered to you in the pursuit of your business. If you are going to have a good credit record, the payment of these invoices must be timely and you will need an efficient system for keeping track of what you owe and when it should be paid. If you do not accumulate unpaid invoices, you may be able to dispense with this record.

6. **Accounts Receivable** — This ledger is used to keep track of debts owed to you by your customers as a result of sale of products or the rendering of services. Each client with an open account should have a separate page with account information. If you do not have open accounts, you will not need this ledger.

7. **Travel & Entertainment Records** — These are the records used to keep track of auto and transportation expenses, meals and entertainment of clients, and travel out of your local area. Due to past abuse in this area, the IRS requires careful documentation as proof that deductions claimed are in fact business related expenses. It is suggested that your travel and entertainment records be organized so they can be carried with you. It is much easier to keep track of them at the time they occur than to try to remember them and find receipts after the fact. Be sure to read the appropriate section on "Travel & Entertainment" in Publication 334, Tax Guide to Small Business.

8. **Customer Records** — These records are kept as a means of helping a business deal more effectively with its customers. The type you keep is purely subjective. They are most effective in service industries or in small businesses dealing in specialty retail sales. An example

of a customer file might be a set of 3 x 5 cards, one for each customer, with specialized information such as name, address, telephone no., services rendered, purchases made, and any other information that will help you to better serve the customer.

9. **Business Checkbook** — The business checkbook is not only the means to pay your bills. It also serves as a record as to whom you paid, how much you paid, and what was purchased. Deposits are recorded here and a balance of cash available is always at your fingertips. It is best to use a desk size checkbook with plenty of space for recording information. Always reconcile your checkbook with your bank statement at the end of each month and record any service charges, checks purchased and interest earned. Your checkbook information will be transferred to the General Journal when you do your weekly bookkeeping.

FINANCIAL STATEMENTS

Financial statements are developed from the general records previously discussed. These statements are used to provide information in preparing tax returns. Even more importantly, the use of those financial statements can help you to see the financial condition of your business and to identify its relative strengths and weaknesses. The business owner who takes the time to understand and evaluate his operation through financial statements over the life of the business will be far ahead of the entrepreneur who concerns himself with only his product or service.

In this chapter we will introduce you to the two principal financial statements of any business—the Balance Sheet and the Profit & Loss Statement.

1. **Balance Sheet** — The balance sheet is a financial statement that shows the condition of the business as of a fixed date. It is usually done at the close of every accounting period. The Balance Sheet can be likened to a **still** photograph. It is the picture of your firms financial condition at a given moment and will show you whether your financial position is strong or weak. Examination of this statement will allow you to analyze your business and implement timely modifications.

The Balance Sheet lists a business' assets, liabilities, and net worth. The Assets are anything your business owns that has monetary value. Liabilities are debts owed by the business to any of its creditors. The Net Worth is an amount equal to the owner's equity. The three are related in that at any given time the business' assets always equal the total contributions of its creditors and owners. This is simply illustrated by the familiar formula:

$$\text{ASSETS} = \text{LIABILITIES} + \text{NET WORTH}$$
OR
$$\text{ASSETS} - \text{LIABILITIES} = \text{NET WORTH}$$

It is apparent from the second formula that if a business possesses more assets than it owes to its creditors (liabilities), its Net Worth will be a positive. Conversely, if the business owes more than it possesses, its Net Worth (or owner equity) will be a negative.

NOTE: A sample balance sheet can be found at the end of the chapter.

2. **Profit & Loss Statement** — This financial statement shows your business financial activity over a specific period of time. It should be prepared at the close of each month. Unlike the Balance Sheet, the Profit & Loss (or income statement) can be likened to a **moving** picture--showing where your money came from and where it was spent over a specific period of time. You will be able to pick out weaknesses in your operation and plan ways to run your business more effectively, thereby increasing your profits.

The Profit & Loss Statement is prepared by transferring totals from your General Journal at the end of the month. At the end of December you will have a moving picture of the revenues and expenses over a 12-month period. Comparison of the Profit & Loss Statements of several years will reveal such trends in your business as high revenue periods, effective advertising months, increases or decreases in profit margin, and a host of other valuable information. Do not underestimate the value of this most important tool.

Just as the Balance Sheet has an accepted format, the Profit & Loss Statement must contain certain categories in a particular order. An example of the financial statement can be seen at the end of the chapter.

GENERAL RECORDKEEPING SCHEDULE

There is a specific order to recordkeeping. It must be done in a timely manner if those records are to be effective. Since the two goals of Recordkeeping are retrieval of tax information and the analyzing of information for internal planning, your schedule will have to provide for these goals. The tasks are listed according to frequency--daily, weekly, monthly, and end of the year. Schedules for filing tax information are not included. They can be found in our book entitled **Recordkeeping: The Secret to Growth & Profit** or in **IRS Publication 334, Tax Guide for Small Business.** For your convenience, we have included a basic General Recordkeeping Schedule on the next page. This schedule may or may not be complete for your particular business needs. However, it should serve to act as a general guide for the person who has no recordkeeping experience.

GENERAL RECORDKEEPING SCHEDULE
(POST FOR YOUR CONVENIENCE)

DAILY

1. File mail in appropriate folders.
2. Unpack and shelve incoming inventory.
3. Record inventory information.
4. Pay any invoices necessary to meet discount deadlines.

WEEKLY

1. Prepare income deposit.
2. Enter deposit in checkbook and General Journal.
3. Enter sales information in Inventory Record.
4. Enter week's checking transactions in General Journal.
5. Record Petty Cash Purchases and file receipts.
6. Pay invoices due. Be aware of discount dates.
7. Enter other purchases in appropriate records, (i.e., fixed assets).

MONTHLY

1. Balance checkbook. (Reconcile with statement)
2. Enter interest earned and bank charges in General Journal and checkbook.
3. Total and balance all General Journal columns.
4. Enter monthly income and expense totals on Profit & Loss Statement.
5. Check Accounts Payable and send out Statements.
6. Prepare monthly Profit & Loss (Income) Statement

END OF YEAR

1. Pay all invoices, sales taxes, and other expenses which you wish to use as deductions for the current year.
2. Transfer 12th month totals from General Journal to Profit & Loss Statement.
3. Total horizontal columns of the Profit & Loss Statement for yearly accounts.
4. Prepare an end-of-the-year Balance Sheet.
5. Using your Profit & Loss Statement, prepare a Budget for next year.
6. Make an appointment with your tax accountant.
7. Set up new records for the coming year.

GENERAL JOURNAL

CHECK #	DATE	TRANSACTION	INCOME	EXPENSE	SALES	S.TAX	REPAIRS	PURCH.	ADVERT.	MISCELL.
		Balance forward--	326 00	172 56	100 00	6 00	220 00	96 00	63 56	13 00
234	7/13	J.J. Advertising		32 00					32 00	
235	7/13	Rutger Products		51 00				51 00		
236	7/16	Regal Stationers		23 42						(off. supp.) 23 42
***	7/17	SALES Taylor	81 70		45 00	2 70				
		Jones			34 00 RESALE					
***	7/17	REPAIRS Davis $20, Jones $35, Smith $85	140 00				140 00			
237	7/19	PETTY CASH DEPOSIT		50 00						50 00
		TOTALS	547 70	328 98	179 00	8 70	360 00	147 00	95 56	86 42

PETTY CASH RECORD

DATE	PURCHASED FROM	EXPENSE ACCT. DEBITED	DEPOSIT		EXPENSE		BALANCE	

Note: 1. Save all receipts for cash purchases!!!
2. Record purchases WEEKLY in Petty Cash Record.
3. File all receipts. These are deductible expenses.
4. Be sure to record your Petty Cash deposits.

INVENTORY RECORD
(IDENTIFIABLE ITEMS)

DATE PURCH.	INVENTORY PURCHASED (description & stock no.)	PURCH. PRICE	BUYER'S NAME	SALE DATE	SALE PRICE	SALES TAX

NOTE: The Inventory Record shown here is to be used for keeping track of goods purchased for resale. Each page should deal with only one type of item or with goods purchased from one wholesaler. Use that company's name as a heading. If you buy like items from several sources, use the type of purchase as a heading. This will make the information easy to retrieve when it is needed. Inventories for your own tools, equipment, etc. do not need the last four columns.

KEEP YOUR INVENTORY CURRENT!!!

INVENTORY RECORD
(NON-IDENTIFIABLE ITEMS)

PRODUCTION OR PURCHASE DATE	DESCRIPTION OF ITEM	NUMBER OF UNITS	UNIT COST	MARKET VALUE ON DATE OF INVENTORY

Note: These items are inventoried by a physical count or by computer records. They are then valued according to rules that apply for FIFO or LIFO. Read the information in your tax guide carefully before determining inventory value.

FIXED ASSETS LOG

ASSETS PURCHASED	PURCH. DATE	PURCH. PRICE	DEPREC. ALLOWED	NO. YRS. TO BE DEPREC.	DATE SOLD	SALE PRICE

Note: See IRS Pub. 334 (Rev. Nov. 87) "Tax Guide for Small Business", (Chapter 12) for more detailed information on depreciation.

The Home-Based Entrepreneur

ACCOUNTS PAYABLE

NAME OF CREDITOR _____

ACCOUNT NO. _____

INVOICE DATE	INVOICE NO.	AMOUNT OF INVOICE		DATE PAID	AMOUNT PAID		BALANCE DUE	

ACCOUNTS RECEIVABLE

NAME OF CUSTOMER_____

ACCOUNT NO._____

INVOICE DATE	INVOICE NO.	INVOICE AMOUNT		TERMS	DATE PAID	AMOUNT PAID		BALANCE	

TRAVEL RECORD

TRIP TO: _____

REASON: _____

DATES: From _____ To _____

DATE	TIME	LOCATION	REASON FOR EXPENSE	COST	

NOTE: 1. You must prove each separate amount you spent for travel away from home, such as the cost of your transportation or lodging.

2. You may total the daily cost of your meals and other incidental elements of such travel if they are listed in reasonable categories, such as meals, gas and oil, and taxi fares.

3. For more information, see IRS Publication 463.

ENTERTAINMENT EXPENSE RECORD

DATES: From_____ To_____

DATE	LOCATION	BUSINESS REASON	CLIENT INFORMATION	BUSINESS REP. PRESENT	COST	

NOTE: 1. For more information on Meals or Entertainment, please refer to IRS Publication 463, "Travel, Entertainment, and Gift Expenses".

The Home-Based Entrepreneur

COMPANY NAME
BALANCE SHEET

_____ __ , 19___

ASSETS

Current Assets

Cash $_____

Petty Cash $_____

Accounts Receivable $_____

Inventory $_____

Short-Term Investments $_____

Prepaid Expenses $_____

Long-Term Investments $_____

Fixed Assets

Land $_____

Buildings $_____

Improvements $_____

Equipment $_____

Furniture $_____

Autos/Vehicles $_____

Other Assets

1. $_____

2. $_____

3. $_____

4. $_____

TOTAL ASSETS $_____

LIABILITIES

Current Liabilities

Accounts Payable $_____

Notes Payable $_____

Interest Payable $_____

Taxes Payable
  Fed. Inc. Tax $_____
  State Inc. Tax $_____
  Self-Emp.Tax $_____
  Sales Tax (SBE) $_____
  Property Tax $_____

Payroll Accrual $_____

Long-Term Liabilities

Notes Payable $_____

TOTAL LIABILITIES $_____

NET WORTH

Proprietorship $_____
or
Partnership
  (Name's) Equity $_____
  (Name's) Equity $_____
or
Corporation
  Capital Stock $_____
  Surplus Paid In $_____
  Retained Earnings $_____

TOTAL NET WORTH $_____

Assets — Liabilities = Net Worth

Total Liabilities and Equity will always be equal to Total Assets!

FOR THE YEAR 19____.

	JAN	FEB	MAR	APR	MAY	JUN	JUL	AUG	SEP	OCT	NOV	DEC
INCOME												
1. Net Sales												
2. Cost of Goods Sold												
3. Gross Profit on Sales												
EXPENSES												
1. Selling Expense (Direct)												
a. ADVERTISING												
b. FREIGHT												
c. PACKAGING COSTS												
d. PARTS & SUPPLIES												
e. SALES SALARIES												
f. MISC. DIRECT EXP.												
2. Admin. Exp. (Indirect)												
a. INSURANCE												
b. LICENSES & PERMITS												
c. OFFICE SALARIES												
d. RENT EXPENSE												
e. UTILITIES												
f. MISCELL. INDIR. EXP.												
g.												
TOTAL EXPENSES												
INCOME FROM OPERATIONS												
OTHER INCOME (Interest)												
OTHER EXPENSE (Interest)												
INCOME BEFORE TAXES												
INCOME TAXES												
NET INCOME												

TAX DEDUCTIONS FOR A HOME-BASED BUSINESS

THE HOME-BASED ENTREPRENEUR

TAX DEDUCTIONS FOR A HOME-BASED BUSINESS

WARNING DISCLAIMER

This chapter presents subject matter with the understanding that we are in no way rendering legal, accounting, or other professional services. The purpose is to introduce you to tax information for home-based businesses. Detailed information, along with legal advice, will have to be obtained from your accountant, attorney, or the IRS.

You may be able to deduct some of the expenses of using part of your **home** for business. The business use of your home, however, must meet specific tests, and your deduction is limited. In this chapter you will learn some of the requirements for taking this deduction and the method for figuring it.

According to the IRS, a home includes a house, apartment, condominium, cooperative, mobile home, boat or similar property. It also includes other structures on the property, such as unattached garage, studio, barn, or greenhouse. However, a home does not include the part of your property that is used exclusively as a hotel, inn, or similar establishment.

HOME BUSINESS USE TESTS

If you separate your business from your home, using a room or other space as an office or area for business activity, you will have to meet certain tests in order to deduct home expenses allocated to your business. These rules apply to self-employed individuals, trusts, estates, partnerships, and S corporation shareholders. They do not apply to corporations.

EXCLUSIVE & REGULAR USE

To take a deduction in using part of your home in business, that part must be used "exclusively" and "regularly":

1. As the principal place of business for any trade or business in which you engage;

2. As a place to meet or deal with your patients, clients or customers in the normal course of your trade or business; or

3. In connection with your trade or business; if you are using a separate structure that is not attached to your home or residence.

WHAT IS EXCLUSIVE USE?

"Exclusive use" means that you must use a specific part of your home only for the purpose of your trade or business. This means you cannot use that portion of your home for a business office and also use it for personal purposes. There are two exceptions to the exclusive use test. They are the use of part of your home for storage of inventory and the use of part of your home as a day-care facility.

1. **Inventory or Storage**- The inventory must be kept for use in your trade or business. That business must be the wholesale or retail selling of products. Your home must be the only fixed location of your trade or business and the storage space must be a separately identifiable space suitable for storage and used on a regular basis.

2. **Day-Care Facility**- If the use of part of your home as a day-care facility is not exclusive, you must figure what part of available time you actually use it for business. For instance, if you use a space for day-care 30% of each day and the space occupies 40% of your home, you will be able to deduct 30% of the expenses that benefit only that area and 12% (30% x 40%) of the expenses you incur for keeping up and running your entire home.

WHAT IS REGULAR USE?

"Regular Use" means that you use the exclusive business part of your home on a continuing basis. The occasional or incidental business use of a part of your home does not meet the regular use test even if that part of your home is not used for any other purpose.

DEDUCTIONS FOR BUSINESS USE OF YOUR HOME

Keep in mind that in this chapter we are targeting only those expenses that relate to the business use of a part of your home. In essence, your home-based business varies from others only in respect to the process that is used to divide the expenses for operating in part of your home between personal use and business use. The expenses that relate to operating a business in a part of your home must be allocated to that business according to the percentage of the total area used, the percentage of time that it is used for the business, and the benefit of that expense to the business portion of your home.

TO FIGURE BUSINESS DEDUCTION PERCENTAGES

To figure deduction for the business use of your home, you have to find the percentage of the total area that is being used for business purposes. This is figured by dividing the area used for business by the total area of your home. (Example- Your home measures 2,000 sq.ft. divided by 500 sq.ft.=25%. You are using 25% of your home for business.)

TIME ALLOCATION OF BUSINESS USE

For those businesses that are not required to meet the "Exclusive Use Test", (for storage of inventory and for the use of part of your home as a day-care facility), the expenses must not only be allocated by percentage of the home used, but by what part of available time you actually use it for business. To do this, compare the total time for business use to the total time that part of your home can be used for all purposes. If, for example, you use part of your home for childcare services on an average of 8 hrs. a day, 5 days a week, for 50 weeks and during the rest of the time that space is used for family use, your time allocation would be as follows:

1. Compute the hours allocated to childcare in one year 8 hours x 5 days x 50 weeks = 2,000 hours.

2. Compute the total usage hours available in one year 24 hours x 365 days = 8,760 hours.

3 .Divide the hours allocated to business usage by the total wage hours available: 2,000 divided by 8,760 = 22.83% Time Allocation to Business Use.

NOTE: If this business uses one-third of the area of the home for childcare, the Indirect Home Maintenance Expenses discussed later on would be computed by multiplying the space allocation percentage (33.33%) x the time allocation percentage (22.83%). The resulting figure (7.61%) would be the allowable deduction of each of these expenses.

HOME MAINTENANCE-WHAT CAN YOU DEDUCT?

Up to this point, you should have learned two things. You now know whether or not you meet the requirements for claiming business use of a part of your home. You also know how to compute the percentage of the total area of your home that is being used for business purposes and, if applicable, how to compute the time allocation of business use of that area. Now it is time to look at the various kinds of expenses you pay to maintain your home. Some expenses are directly related to the business, others are indirectly related, and some are unrelated. Each of these three types of expenses will be discussed in the following text.

DIRECT HOME MAINTENANCE EXPENSES

Direct home maintenance expenses are those that benefit only the business part of your home. They include painting or repairs made to the specific area or room that is used for business. You may deduct directly related expenses in full. For example, if you spend $500.00 to paint the area that contains your business, the full amount is deductible.

NOTE: If you use the business area to provide day-care services or use it less than exclusively for inventory, expenses for that part of your home are subject to time allocation and also to the "deduction limitation" to be discussed later.

INDIRECT HOME MAINTENANCE EXPENSES

Indirect home maintenance expenses are those expenses you have for keeping up and running your entire home. They benefit both the business and the personal parts of your home. They include the following:

1. **Real Estate** - If you own your home, you may deduct part of the real estate tax you pay on your home as a business expense. Multiply the total tax by the percentage of your home used for business.

2. **Deductible Mortgage Interest** - You may deduct part of any home mortgage interest as a business expense. This includes interest on a second trust. To figure the business part that is deductible, multiply the mortgage interest by the percentage of your home used for business.

3. **Casualty Losses** - If the loss is on property used for both business and personal purposes, only the business part is a business deduction. If the loss is sustained on property used only in your business, the entire loss is treated as a business deduction. If the loss is on the portion of your property not used in your business, there is no allowable deduction. (See IRS Publication 5478 549)

4. **Rent** - If you rent your home, rather than own one, the part of the rent applicable to business use is deductible. Multiply the total rent by the percentage of your home used for business.

5. **Utilities and Services** - This includes such expenses as electricity, gas, trash removal, and cleaning services. They are primarily personal, but the percentage that can be attributed to the business part of your home is deductible. The percentage is usually the same as the percentage of your home used for business.

6. **Insurance** - You may deduct the cost of insurance that covers the business part of your home. Be sure to deduct only the portion of the premium that applies to the current tax year.

7. **Repairs** - Repairs keep your home in good working order over its useful life. Examples of common repairs are patching walls and floors, painting, wallpapering, repairing roofs and gutters, and mending leaks. Multiply the cost of repairs and supplies-- including labor, other than your own-- by the percentage of the area of your home used for business.

8. **Security System** - Expenses you incur to maintain or monitor the system are deductible. Multiply the total expense by the percentage of area used for business.

   NOTE: The cost of the system is deducted under depreciation expense.

9. **Depreciation** - The cost of property with a useful life of more than one year, such as a building, a permanent improvement, or furniture is a capital expenditure. That cost generally may not be deducted entirely in one year.

   NOTE: Depreciation expense is figured on Form 4562 "Depreciation and Amortization," according to one of several methods. See Publication 534, "Depreciation".

UNRELATED EXPENSES

Unrelated expenses are expenses that benefit only the parts of your home that you *do not* use for business. These include repairs to personal areas of your home, lawn care, and landscaping. You cannot deduct unrelated expenses. In addition, no deduction is allowed for the fair rental value of your home.

HOME OFFICE DEDUCTION LIMITATION

There is a limit on the amount of otherwise nondeductible expenses, such as utilities, insurance, and depreciation that may be taken for business use of your home. The total of these deductions, (with depreciation taken last), cannot exceed the net income derived from that use.

NOTE:

1. There is no limitation on expenses you may deduct for the business use of your home if your total expenses, including depreciation, are less than or equal to your gross income from that business use.

2. If you realize no income during the tax year, no deduction is allowed.

DETERMINING THE DEDUCTION LIMITATION

The limitations on further deductions can best be seen by using the following example: ABC Products is a wholesale product business operating out of a home. 25% of that home is used exclusively and regularly for the business. Computation of the Deduction Limitation might read as follows:

Gross Receipts on Wholesale Sales	$50,000
Less Cost of Goods Sold	20,000
Gross Income from Business	$30,000
Less deductible mortgage interest, real estate taxes, and casualty losses-(25% only).	8,000
BALANCE	$22,000
Less business expenses that could be claimed if you did not have a home office-(salaries, bus, phone, etc.)	15,000
Gross Income Limit (not less than zero)	$ 7,000
Less other expenses allocable to business use of home-(25%).	
1. Maintenance, utilities, repairs, insurance, etc.	5,000
LIMIT ON FURTHER DEDUCTION	$ 2,000
2. Less Depreciation	6,000
Amount Carried Over to Next Year	
(subject to income limitations)	$ 4,000

The next page contains a blank worksheet to help you figure the deductions for a business use of a home. The last two pages of the chapter is a list of free IRS publications that will prove helpful to you as a business owner. Publication 587, "Business Use of Your Home", specifically targets the home-based entrepreneur. **NOTE: Please do not hesitate to seek further help from a qualified tax expert!**

TAX WORK SHEET

BUSINESS USE OF YOUR HOME

Worksheet for Figuring the Deduction for Business Use of a Home

Step 1—Part of your home used for business:

Part A. Area basis (part used exclusively)

1) Area of home used for business   1)_____
2) Total area of home   2)_____
3) Percentage of home used for business (divide line 1 by line 2)   3)_____

Part B. Time usage basis (part used to provide day-care services)

4) Total hours facility used (days x   hrs.)   4)_____
5) Total hours available (24 hrs. x 366 days)   5)_____8784_____
6) Percentage of time used for business (divide line 4 by line 5)   6)_____
7) Percentage of home used for business (multiply line 6 by line 3)   7)_____

Step 2—Figuring your gross income limit:

8a) Gross receipts from business use of your home: 8a)_____
    b) Less returns and allowances   8b)_____
    c) Less cost of goods sold   8c)_____
9) **Gross income from business**   9)_____
10) Enter in **Business part** the **Total expenses** multiplied by the business percentage as figured in a reasonable allocation such as line 3 or line 7, if applicable:

	Total expense	Business part
a) Deductible mortgage interest	10a)_____	_____
b) Real estate taxes	10b)_____	_____
c) Casualty losses	10c)_____	_____

d) Total of (a) through (c). Subtract line 10(d) from line 9, but do not enter less than zero (–0–)   10d)_____
e) **Balance**   10e)_____
11) Less other business expenses not attributable to unit (salaries, business phone, etc.)   11)_____
12) **Gross income limit** (but not less than zero)   12)_____

Step 3—Business part of expenses attributable to the unit

13) Enter in **Business part** the **Total expenses** multiplied by the business percentage as figured in a reasonable allocation such as line 3 or line 7, if applicable:

	Total expense	Business part
a) Utilities	13a)_____	_____
b) Insurance	13b)_____	_____
c) Maintenance	13c)_____	_____
d) Repairs	13d)_____	_____
e) Excess mortgage interest	13e)_____	_____
f) Other expenses	13f)_____	_____

g) Total of (a) through (f), plus carryover from last year   13g)_____

If line 13(g) is equal to or less than line 12, subtract line 13(g) from line 12, enter the balance here, and go on to Step 4. If line 12 is zero, enter -0- on line 13(h) and carry over the excess on line 13(g), along with any excess amount in Step 4, to next year. If line 13(g) exceeds line 12, deduct only those expenses equal to line 12. You must carry over the excess expense to next year, along with any excess from Step 4. **Balance** (if any)[1]   13h)_____

Step 4—Depreciation and excess casualty loss

14) Excess casualty loss ($100 plus 10% of your adjusted gross income):   14)_____
15) Figuring depreciation for your home (use Form 4562 or the table below)[2]:
    a) Adjusted basis of home   15a)_____
    b) Less—land   15b)_____
    c) Basis of building   15c)_____
    d) Business percentage (line 3 or line 7, above, whichever applies)   15d)_____
    e) **Business** basis of building (multiply line (c) by line (d))   15e)_____
    f) ACRS (or MACRS) percentage or other method of depreciation   15f)_____
    g) Depreciation allowable (multiply line (e) by line (f)), or from Form 4562, plus last year's carryover   15g)_____

Add lines 14 and 15(g) and enter the total on line 15(h). If line 15(h) is equal to or less than line 13(h), deduct line 15(h) from line 13(h) and enter the balance here. If line 15(h) exceeds line 13(h), deduct only an amount equal to line 13(h). You must carry over the excess to next year.[1]   15h)_____
     15i)_____

[1] Any excess amount on lines 13(g) and 15(h) carried over to next year is subject to the gross income limit (line 12 of worksheet) for that year.

[2] See Publication 534, *Depreciation*, for more information on figuring depreciation.

☆ U. S. GOVERNMENT PRINTING OFFICE: 1988 242-484/80044

8

FREE PUBLICATIONS
AVAILABLE FROM THE IRS

The following is a list of the publications referred to in the preceding material, along with others which may prove helpful to you in the course of your business. Make it a point to keep a file of tax information. Send for these publications and update your file with new publications at least once a year. The United States Government has spent a great deal of time and money to make this information available to you for preparation of income tax returns.

Information on ordering these publications can be found following this listing. Or if you prefer, you may call IRS toll free at [1 (800) 424-3676].

For a complete listing, see Publication 910, *Guide to Tax Free Services*.

> 334 - *Tax Guide for Small Business*
> 910 - *Guide to Free Tax Services*

Begin by reading the three publications listed above. They will give you the most comprehensive information. Others which may be helpful are:

> 15 - *Circular E., Employer's Tax Guide*
> 463 - *Travel, Entertainment & Gift Expenses*
> 505 - *Tax Withholding & Estimated Tax*
> 508 - *Educational Expenses*
> 509 - *Tax Calendars for 1988*
> 533 - *Self-Employment Tax*
> 534 - *Depreciation*
> 535 - *Business Expenses*
> 536 - *Net Operating Losses*
> 538 - *Accounting Periods & Methods*
> 539 - *Employment Taxes*
> 541 - *Taxes on Partnerships*
> 542 - *Tax Information on Corporations*
> 545 - *Deduction for Bad Debts*
> 557 - *Tax-Exempt Status for Your Organization*
> 560 - *Self-Employed Retirement Plans*
> 583 - *Information for Business Taxpayers*
> 587 - *Business Use of Your Home*
> 589 - *Tax Information on S Corporations*
> 596 - *Earned Income Credit*
> 908 - *Bankruptcy*
> 911 - *Tax Information for Direct Sellers*
> 916 - *Information Returns (Non-employee payments)*
> 917 - *Business Use of a Car*
> 921 - *Explanation of the Tax Reform Act for Business*
> 925 - *Passive Activity & At Risk Rules*

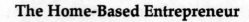

INSURANCE
CONSIDERATIONS

THE HOME-BASED ENTREPRENEUR

INSURANCE CONSIDERATIONS

Insurance helps safeguard your business against losses from fire, injury, and illness. It allows the owner to reduce the risk of loss due to circumstances beyond his control and lets him concentrate on making a success of the business.

The confusion and costs surrounding insurance should not deter the owner from protecting a new or growing enterprise. The first step is to identify the risks of the business which need to be covered and project the largest amount of possible loss. Second, the owner must become aware of the basic types of insurance available. Most businesses should evaluate the following basic types of insurance.

LIABILITY INSURANCE

This type of insurance protects the business from financial loss due to lawsuits resulting from bodily injury or property damage. **Professional liability insurance** should be purchased by those in professions where malpractice could result in litigation. Examples would be opticians, doctors, dentists, accountants, beauticians, and lawyers. **Product liability insurance** protects you in case your product causes injury to the user. Liability insurance can be one of the most expensive types of insurance. One way to reduce costs is to exclude the coverage in a comprehensive package which does not apply to your business. Also, membership in trade and professional associations may allow you to take advantage of group insurance benefits.

PROPERTY AND FIRE INSURANCE

This coverage offers protection against damage to or loss of equipment or inventory and business interruption caused by fire, theft, vandalism, explosion, or windstorm. In some areas, earthquake coverage is available. Check with the insurance carrier on your homeowner's policy and make sure that the business use of your home is compatible with your policy.

HEALTH INSURANCE

Individual health care policies can be quite expensive. A good option to lower your health insurance costs might be to join a group pooling arrangement which spreads the risk over a large group of people. Frequently, state and local Chambers of Commerce, trade associations, and professional organizations offer group medical policies.

WORKMAN'S COMPENSATION INSURANCE

Provides for benefits to employees who may be injured on the job. This type of insurance is required by law and premiums vary according to the occupation and salaries of the employees.

AUTOMOBILE INSURANCE

Provides property and liability coverage for vehicles owned by the business or vehicles used for business purposes. Business use is excluded under personal auto insurance policies,so if your personal vehicle will be used for business purposes, you will be required to secure additional auto liability insurance. Discuss this issue with your insurance carrier.

DISABILITY INSURANCE

This provides a form of health insurance which protects your income in case you become disabled.

BUSINESS LIFE INSURANCE

Coverage can provide funds for transition when an owner or partner dies.

These are some of the basic types of insurance to be considered by business owners. Talk to your insurance representative about your business needs. Shop around and evaluate your personal needs. Final advice for the wise business owner is to read and understand the policy, especially the fine print and to reevaluate your business insurance needs every six months.

MARKET
RESEARCH

THE HOME-BASED ENTREPRENEUR

MARKET RESEARCH

In order to be successful, a business must know its market. Market research involves finding out if there is a need for your product or service **before** committing a great deal of time and money to the project. It involves finding out what a customer wants and needs and determining how your company can meet those wants and needs.

THE USE OF QUESTIONNAIRES

A cost-effective method of gaining a response from the market regarding your product or service is through the use of a **questionnaire.** Surveys are an excellent means of determining the response to what you have to offer and a questionnaire is the most common means of collecting data. A questionnaire begins with an introduction. Explain the nature of your business. Describe your product or your service and tell what is unique about it and how it will benefit the customer. Your initial contact with the reader is established in the opening statement. A well-designed questionnaire can gather data covering four main areas: (1) Interest in your product or service, (2) Demographics, (3) The means for reaching your market, and (4) The competition.

1. **Interest in your product or service** — For example, include questions aimed at determining a need for your product or service. ("Would you be interested in home-delivery of gourmet meals?" "Would you be interested in a gift buying service?" "Are you looking for housekeeping services?")

2. **Demographics** — Questions can be structured to show you the kind of people your prospects are. These questions gather the demographic and psychographic information on your market. ("Do you work away from your home city?" "Do you shop where you work?" "Do you shop where you live?" "What price would you expect to pay for this product?" "What would you expect to pay for this service?" "What is your age range?" "What is your household income?" "Do you own or rent your home?")

3. **The Means for Reaching Your Market** — Questions can be included which will show you how to reach your customers. ("What newspapers do you read?" "What radio stations do you listen to?" "What TV programs do you watch?" "Do you use discount coupons?" "Do you order through catalogs?" "Where would you expect to buy this product?")

4. **The Competition** — Questions about the competition can show you ways in which your company can be unique and can benefit the customer. ("What company do you currently use?" "What do you like about their product or service?" "How can the product or service be improved?")

REACHING YOUR QUESTIONNAIRE MARKET

Give the questionnaire to valid, potential customers, not family and friends. Your market can be contacted through the mail, by telephone, or through personal or group interviews. You may rent a mailing list, use a geographical phone directory, conduct interviews through clubs and organizations. Display tables at community events are a good way to make contact with the buying public and gather information.

EVALUATING TRENDS IN YOUR INDUSTRY

Evaluate the trends in your industry. Contact trade and professional associations in your field to determine the demand for the product or service you are considering. These entities are also good resources for gathering information on current acceptable pricing levels. Trade journals often forecast trends and indicate new products and services before they hit the market. This information could give you the leading edge. Your attendance at trade shows will also introduce you to new products and services, give you indications of consumer demand, and allow you to meet with suppliers.

EVALUATION OF THE COMPETITION

Another important part of market research is the evaluation of the **competition.** Your questionnaire results may have indicated the competition in the area in which you plan to do business. The phone directories, Business License Bureau, and trade & professional directories will list other competitors.

If you are going into a service business, the competition can be evaluated by posing as a customer. Call or visit the shop and ask about job rates, delivery service, terms of payment, discount policies, and warranties or guarantees.

You may make use of the competitor's service in order to give it a rating. Try to determine the good points which you will take to your company. Learn from the weaknesses of the competition and make them your strengths.

If you are developing a product line, visit shops where products similar to yours are displayed. Are the sales clerks knowledgeable? Does the packaging explain the product? Where is the product displayed? What seems to be the turn-over rate? Has it been recently been marked down? Your trade and professional associations can give you information on the normal wholesale and mark-up rate for your industry. Knowing this, you can evaluate the wholesale cost of the competition's products by taking a percentage of the retail price.

PRICING YOUR PRODUCT OR SERVICE

One of the major considerations in market research is determining a price for your product or service. As business owners, we price a product at what we **want** it to sell for, rather than at what it **will** sell for. There are two important factors to keep in mind when developing a pricing structure.

1. **Price Ceiling** - The first is to recognize that it is the **market** and not your costs that determine the price at which a product will sell. You will need to determine the "price ceiling" or the top price a customer will pay for your product. Market research will help you arrive at that figure. Your questionnaires will show what a customer will expect to pay. The information from trade and professional organizations will indicate pricing trends and guidelines. Evaluation of the pricing structure of your competition will indicate what the market is currently paying. The principal to remember is that products (or services) are bought on the basis of perceived value in the minds of buyers, and not on the basis of what it costs you to produce or purchase a product.

2. **Price Floor** - Even though the cost of your product or service is not directly related to what the customer is willing to pay for it, costs are of extreme importance to you, as the business owner. You must be aware of how much it costs you to produce your product or to provide your service. This means that you must take into account all of the operating and other expenses of the business. You must also know your desired annual net profit. How much do you need to make to feel that your

business has been profitable? Evaluation of your costs and your desired profits allow you to establish a "price floor"--the price below which you cannot sell and make the necessary profit.

OPERATING BETWEEN THE PRICE FLOOR AND PRICE CEILING

Successful businesses operate between their price floor and price ceiling. The next chapter will show how to work with the market research information you have gathered on determining an acceptable price for your product or service. You will be able to see how the pricing and costing information can be combined to determine the viability of your business. Careful research and the development of a business plan can and will help you to avoid costly errors and possible business failure.

BUSINESS VIABILITY

COSTING/PRICING
YOUR PRODUCT OR SERVICE

THE HOME-BASED ENTREPRENEUR

BUSINESS VIABILITY
COSTING/PRICING
YOUR PRODUCT OR SERVICE

Unfortunately, a large percentage of new businesses are doomed to failure from the start because their owners have not taken the time to **realistically** project their revenues and expenses. There is a simple and straightforward method that you can use to determine whether or not your product or service is a candidate for a profitable business venture. That determination will require some diligence and a basic understanding about pricing and costing and the application of a simple mathematical formula.

When it comes to business, an overwhelming majority of entrepreneurs fall into the novice category. They have thought of products or services that may or may not revolutionize the world. Their enthusiasm is unparalleled--until they suddenly discover that getting their idea into the marketplace is a business--and that it will require a lot of hard work and planning. Furthermore, if the entrepreneur is going to need outside funding, it would be a rare instance to find a lender or a venture capitalist who will finance that dream solely because both parties think that it is a wonderful idea. Instead, the entrepreneur will have to do the groundwork to convince the buyer, licensee, lender, or venture capitalist that the idea is worthy of his or her attention.

How, then, do you take your idea from the drawing board to the marketplace? There is only one reasonable route to choose. The day has arrived to write a **business plan**. It is the first thing that buyers or investors will want to see. More importantly, it is your blueprint to success. The task is formidable, but it can be accomplished by you. It is a step-by-step process of planning that will eliminate the guesswork for both you and your investors. It is easy and very tempting to figment and lie to yourself and your potential lenders about the cost of your product or service, the projected selling price, and the size of your market. However, the projections and statistics arrived at during the business planning process will result in a more realistic picture and will enable you to determine, in fact, whether or not your idea has the ingredients necessary to become a viable business.

We have promised you a way to determine the viability of your venture. For that purpose, we would like to target two critical projections that will emerge by the time you have completed your business plan.

1. **The true cost of your product or service.**
2. **The selling price of your product or service.**

THE COST OF YOUR PRODUCT

The most common error--and one that will turn your dream into a nightmare--is the failure to account for **all** the costs that are involved in producing your product or service and taking it into the marketplace. Unfortunately, many entrepreneurs come out of business workshops with the mistaken idea that costing encompasses only those expenses relating directly to their products or services and nothing more. The truth is that the cost of your product includes all of the expenses involved in conducting your business. They are as follows:

Cost of Goods to be Sold — Purchase price or cost of manufacturing your product (materials + labor).

Direct Expenses — Those expenses directly related to your product or service. (for example: advertising, delivery vehicle expenses, freight, product development, production and service salaries, selling commissions, supplies, miscell. direct expenses)

Indirect Expenses — Normal office overhead or administrative expenses. (ex: licenses and permits, office supplies, office salaries, maintenance, rents, miscell. taxes, utilities, depreciation expense, professional fees, etc.)

Other Expenses — Interest expense (ie: interest on loans).

Tax Expense — Federal Income Tax, State Income Tax, and Self-Employment Tax (your contribution to Social Security).

Failure to include any of the above expenses in costing your product or service will result in a false projection as to the validity of your business. The projected figures for the above costs are arrived at through researching like businesses, utilizing past financial statements of your own business, or a combination of both.

THE SELLING PRICE OF YOUR PRODUCT OR SERVICE

The information presented in Chapter 11, "Market Research", should have left you with a clear understanding of "price ceiling" and "price floor". If you will recall, **the "price ceiling" of your product or service is dependent on what the market will bear.** It does no good to determine what you want it to sell for if your customers will not pay the price. Selling price is arrived at through marketing studies involving questionnaires, demographics, psychographics, competition analysis, industry trend studies, and market evaluations. Once the selling price has been determined, you will have to project the sales or service volume for your business. For a product oriented business, this is estimated in number of units to be sold. For a service business, volume is in terms of working hours. Projected revenues for your business, then, would be as follows:

FOR A PRODUCT

Net sales = No. Units to be Sold x Selling Price per Unit

FOR A SERVICE

Service Income = No. Working Hours x Hourly Rate

DETERMINING YOUR BUSINESS PROFITABILITY

The viability of your business can only be determined by combining the two ingredients discussed above. If the cost of conducting your business makes it feasible to sell a reasonable number of units of that product or service at a selling price that the market will bear and still leave you with an acceptable net profit after taxes, you are ready to move forward. If the selling price will not yield the desired profit, you will have to return to the drawing board. You **cannot** raise the selling price. Therefore, your options are to increase your revenues, reduce your costs, satisfy yourself with a smaller profit, or give up the idea of turning your idea into a business.

PUTTING TOGETHER A PICTURE OF YOUR BUSINESS

Now that you understand the key elements of costing your product, determining a selling price, and estimating volume of revenue, you are ready to formulate a clear picture of what your business will look like at the end of a taxable year. This is best accomplished by compiling a **One-Year Projection (or Pro Forma Income Statement).** This financial statement interprets all your business and marketing research into readable figures that will enable you to realistically analyze your chances of business success. The Pro Forma Income Statement is a part of the Financial Section of your Business Plan. An example of this statement for both a product and service business follows. For these two examples, let us assume that the projections are these:

	JAN'S T-SHIRTS	BOB'S AUTO REPAIR
Net Sales	$200,000 (10,000 units @ $20.00)	$200,000 (4,000 hrs @ $50.00)
Costs of Goods Sold	50,000 ($2.00 Labor + $3.00 Mat.)	20,000 (Parts Consumed)
Direct (Selling) Expense	25,000	32,000
Indirect (Admin.) Expense	23,000	36,000
Interest Income	500	600
Interest Expense	2,500	12,600

ONE-YEAR PROJECTION
(PRO FORMA INCOME STATEMENT)

	JAN'S T-SHIRTS	BOB'S AUTO REPAIR
INCOME		
1. Net Sales	$200,000	$200,000
2. Cost of Goods Sold	50,000	-20,000
3. Gross Profit on Sales	$150,000	$180,000
EXPENSES		
1. Direct (Selling) Expense	-25,000	-32,000
2. Indirect (Admin.) Expense	-23,000	-36,000
INCOME FROM OPERATIONS	$102,000	$112,000
OTHER INCOME (Interest Inc.)	+500	+600
OTHER EXPENSE (Interest Exp.)	-2,500	-12,600
NET PROFIT (LOSS) BEF.TAXES	$100,000	$100,000
TAXES: 1. Fed. Income Tax	-28,000	-28,000*
2. State Income Tax	-9,000	-9,000*
3. Self-Employment Tax	-6,250	-6,250*
NET PROFIT (LOSS) AFT.TAXES	**$56,750**	**$56,750**

*Tax amounts vary according to current State & Federal schedules. The above amounts are based on 1989 rate projections for a single taxpayer/sole proprietor in California.

FORMULA FOR MANUFACTURERS

Remember that the selling price of your product is determined by what the market will bear. If, after making all of the projections for your product business, you find that you cannot sell your product for that price and still net an acceptable amount, you can work within the framework of this **FORMULA FOR MANUFACTURERS**, increasing or decreasing its components to arrive at the desired selling price.

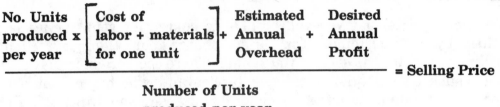

$$\frac{\text{No. Units produced} \times \left[\text{Cost of labor + materials for one unit}\right] + \text{Estimated Annual Overhead} + \text{Desired Annual Profit}}{\text{Number of Units produced per year}} = \text{Selling Price}$$

Using the information from Jan's Projected Income Statement, and assuming that she desires a $50,000 net profit at the end of the year, the formula would compute as follows:

A. $$\frac{10,000 \times (\$2.00 + \$3.00) + \$93,250 + \$50,000}{10,000} = \text{Selling Price}$$

B. $$\frac{\$50,000 + \$92,859 + \$50,000}{10,000} = \$19.32 \text{ Selling Price}$$

Market research has shown that Jan's customers will pay $20.00 for her product. The formula proves that she can reach her desired net profit at a selling price that is 68¢ below her limit. This will give her some leeway if she finds that she exceeds her budget in some areas or if her sales do not quite meet her projections. Her business is viable.

If the computations had proved that Jan's selling price would have to be higher than $20.00, working with this formula will lower that selling price. To decrease the selling price she can do any one or a combination of the following:

1. **Increase number of units to be produced per year.**
2. **Decrease cost of labor per unit.**
3. **Decrease cost of materials per unit.**
4. **Lower annual overhead.**
5. **Decrease desired annual profit.**

I have used the above formula in many classes to make a quick projection for a potential entrepreneur. It is surprising how quickly it becomes obvious that many visions of profitability are only in the mind. When the formula is applied, the entrepreneur is forced to return to the planning process to take a more realistic look at what he must do before taking his product to the marketplace.

HOURLY RATE FORMULA

The hourly rate that you will be able to charge for your service is determined by your customer. You cannot charge more than your clients are willing to pay for the service you render. There are variables that come into play, such as the quality of your service and whether or not you have something unique to offer. In general, however, you will not be able to exceed the norms for your industry. After you have made all of the projections for your service business, you can use the following **HOURLY RATE FORMULA** to arrive at the necessary hourly rate while still maintaining an acceptable net profit.

$$\frac{\textbf{Desired Annual Net Income} \, ^+ \, \textbf{Annual Expenses}}{\textbf{Number of Billable Hours Per Year}} = \textbf{REQUIRED HOURLY RATE}$$

For the purpose of this example, I will use the information from Bob's Projected Income Statement. However, let us also assume that Bob will not be satisfied unless he has a net income of $75,000. This change will also cause a change in Annual Expenses because he will have to have a higher pre-tax figure and his taxes will increase. The formula would compute as follows:

A. $\dfrac{\$75,000 + \$153,209}{4,000}$ = Required Hourly Rate

B. $\dfrac{\$228,209}{4,000}$ = **$57.05 Required Hourly Rate**

Bob has already found through his planning that he can charge no more than $50.00 an hour for his services. If he holds firmly to his requirements for net income, and if he cannot produce more units of work, then the hourly rate he will have to charge will place him out of the market. In order to make his business viable, he will **have** to lower the required hourly rate.

This can be done by decreasing or increasing the various components of the formula as follows:

1. **Decrease Desired Annual Net Income.**
2. **Decrease Annual Expenses.**
3. **Increase Number of Working Hours Per Year.**

In Bob's case, he might be able to hire a part-time mechanic, increasing his labor output by 1,000 hours. This would increase his revenues by 25% while increasing his expenses by only about 15%, yielding him his desired net income of $75,000 and, at the same time, keeping his hourly rate down to the necessary $50.00 as seen in the example below.

$$\frac{\$75,000 + \$176,190}{5,000} = \$50.23 \text{ Required Hourly Rate}$$

MYTH VS. FACT

Before careful planning, it might appear that Jan's T-shirts would cost only $50,000 to produce and $25,000 to sell--which would leave her with a tidy profit of $125,000. By the same token, Bob may envision his auto service expenses to be about $52,000. He would also have in mind a profit of $148,000. With realistic projections, however, both myths are soon dispelled. Jan and Bob would readily see that their net profits after taxes would both be reduced to $56,250 — a decrease of $68,250 for Jan and a decrease of $91,250 for Bob from their initial "guesstimates". It should now be obvious that Business Planning is of primary importance in determining the viability of your entrepreneurial venture. Writing that plan is a simple step-by-step process. It does take time, but can be accomplished through research and logical thinking. Once it is written, you can continue to evaluate your business if you will keep your plan up-to-date and periodically perform a financial analysis.

Remember this — **PLANNING IS YOUR BUSINESS! IT IS THE BEST INSURANCE FOR YOUR SUCCESS!**

PROMOTING AND ADVERTISING A HOME-BASED BUSINESS

THE HOME-BASED ENTREPRENEUR

PROMOTING AND ADVERTISING A HOME-BASED BUSINESS

Promoting and advertising are vital parts of the marketing process. Promotion covers all the techniques that call attention to your business. Advertising is a form of mass communication that you purchase as a substitute for personal selling. Marketing includes identifying your customers, determining the demand for your product or service in the most likely area, evaluating the competition, selecting the most profitable marketing method, developing a business plan, and planning a promotional package that includes everything from business stationary to media advertising.

To plan an effective and appropriate promotion, you must have a thorough knowledge of what it costs you in time, money, and personal energy to conduct your business. You need sound information about all these factors to help you allocate costs of promotion effectively and economically. The information on advertising costs and promotional expenses researched in this chapter would be incorporated into formulas in the previous chapter to help determine a price for your product or an hourly rate for your service business.

One of your first marketing considerations will be to identify your customer base. Without a customer, there is no market. A home-based operator should gain some knowledge about the buying practices of various groups. We used to be concerned only with demographic information, the statistical information dealing with age, sex, race, and income. Now we are also concerned with psychographics or life-style studies. These studies are concerned with buying habits, self-concept, and personal behavior and have more relevance in profiling the customer. Research data can be obtained from libraries, university business departments, trade journals, the Chamber of Commerce, and government agencies such as the Small Business Administration.

Promotion is the way to let people know what your product or service can do for them. Promotional tools include salesmanship, publicity, public relations techniques, memberships in business organizations, trade shows, and paid advertising.

SALESMANSHIP

Selling involves direct contact with customers or through wholesalers or manufacturers representatives. Not everyone is endowed with the natural ability to explain the benefits of a product or service to a potential customer. The art of selling is the ability to understand the needs of a customer and to translate that understanding into the development of a product or service which can be exchanged for money. To effectively promote a business, you must understand that business, believe in its benefits, and be able to communicate those benefits to the market with enthusiasm and conviction.

Home-based businesses differ from larger companies in many ways. One critical difference is the opportunity for the small owner-operated business to provide personalized service to the customer. It is important to earn the trust of the potential buyer. Selling yourself as an individual who provides quality service is as important as selling the benefits of the product or service you provide. Your goal is to create a customer, not merely a sale.

Although many product oriented home-based businesses sell directly to the customer, many others use an indirect distribution method called wholesaling. Successful salesmanship to a wholesale customer requires your understanding of the wholesaler's needs such as seasonal needs and prompt order fulfillment. Wholesale customers are interested in your dependability and integrity as a supplier.

Good salesmanship is dependent on the identity and image you establish for your business. Approach your customers, clients, and wholesalers in a professional manner, present a product or service tailored to their needs, and stand behind your work. As your good reputation grows, so will your market.

PUBLICITY

Publicity is free communication. It differs from paid advertising because there is little or no control over the message that is communicated. You can target advertising because you have paid for a highly specific message. Publicity depends upon someone's having a selective interest in your activities and a willingness to promote them. For example, if you provide a unique service or product, the local media will be interested in doing a feature. Call the local television and radio talk programs and newspapers in your area. Ask if they will be doing a feature on your area of expertise. If not, suggest that they do and offer your services as an expert in the field. You may be interviewed or may submit an article for publication.

The most effective form of publicity is word-of-mouth recommendations from clients. Satisfied customers who tell their friends, relatives, and business associates about your business help to establish your credibility as a business person.

PUBLIC RELATIONS TECHNIQUES

This form of promotion includes displays, community involvements, and personal contacts. They can encompass all promotional efforts including those that are not directly linked to making a sale. Focusing on those aspects of business relations that permit the desired image of your business is most beneficial. Public relations efforts allow you to have greater control in creating a desired image than general publicity because you are able to direct those efforts.

Displays are an excellent way to present your business to the outside world and may be set up at community-oriented functions such as city fairs, community meetings, and civic events.

Community involvement is important for the owner of a home-based business since there is a tendency for the owner to become isolated. Presenting information and examples concerning your business to a community organization is a public relations technique that keeps a home-business owner in touch and visible. If you have started a business that has added a few jobs to the community, the Chamber of Commerce will be interested in learning about your experiences. Membership in civic organizations can pave the way to being a guest speaker. Active membership alone, affords you an excellent opportunity for networking.

Networking is the exchange of ideas and information that takes place every day in your life. You are going to direct that exchange to your benefit and the benefit of those around you. The more you meet with people and network, the more you will be able to promote your business, to learn more about the business community around you, and to become more self-confident.

MEMBERSHIP IN BUSINESS ASSOCIATIONS

Belonging to the right organizations provides opportunities to meet potential customers through sponsored events. Additional customers can be contacted through the networking that takes place during these shows. Members may also share experiences, advice, ideas, and information about their business practices and techniques. Publications and trade journals offer sound advice and valuable information on the state of business.

TRADE SHOWS AND EXHIBITS

Participating, as well as attending, targeted trade shows and exhibits allows you to take advantage of promotional campaigns that would be too expensive to undertake. You can request listings of trade events from local and regional malls. Join your local business organizations and participate in sidewalk sales, street fairs, and other group promotional efforts that are appropriate to your business. These shows are usually only attended by those interested in your particular business or service. This is an excellent way to reach your market.

ADVERTISING

Your advertising plan should be a vital part of your marketing plan. You have an excellent service or a useful product, and you need to let people know what you have to offer. People learn about your business through advertising. Because successful advertising is creative and innovative, the creative person has a distinct advantage in developing an effective strategy.

Advertising can be expensive, so you must be specific in identifying the objectives of your plan. Each home-based business is unique, but the fundamental objectives for advertising should include creating a public awareness of your business, reaching new customers, increasing sales and profits, and being cost-effective.

The first step is to define potential customers in the geographic area served by your business. Do some preliminary surveys and interviews to determine which means of advertising will reach them. What newspapers do they read? Which radio stations do they listen to? Do they use discount coupons? Do they respond to direct mail? Tailor your advertising efforts to your market.

With a home-based business you must operate within the local codes when advertising. You also need to consider the security of your home. Calling attention to your business may make your home and family vulnerable to crime.

When you know which audience you want to reach and where you want the information to appear, you must look at the various methods of advertising available to you. Advertising methods differ according to medium, complexity, target audience, and cost. Some forms of advertising are more effective for a home-based business than others.

> **Newspaper Advertising** is fairly effective for a small business. A relatively large number of people can be reached through a classified ad. Display ads are more costly and should be placed in the newspaper section read by your market. The cost of your ad will vary according to the circulation areas and the frequency of publication.

> **Direct Mail** is fairly costly but may be economical in the long run because it delivers specific information in a personal way to large numbers of people. If you operate a mail-order business, direct mail advertising is especially appropriate because

you can target your advertising. Direct mail can be used to distribute letters, promotional give-aways, discount coupons, and brochures.

Brochures can be expensive but they are essential for any business for which the prospective customer needs detailed information about the qualifications and expertise of the owner and the services and products offered. More information can be supplied in a brochure than would be practical for a classified ad. Brochures can be mailed, distributed door to door, or given out at community events and trade shows.

Yellow Page Directories should not be overlooked as a means of advertising. Every person with a telephone has a copy of the Yellow Pages. Directories are one of the most widely-used forms of advertising. The telephone company advertising staff will give you help in designing an ad which will present your business in an effective manner. Be aware that directories are published at various times of the year. Call the phone company to determine the publication deadlines. A home-based business may wish to omit the address from the ad. Phone calls can be screened and clients can be scheduled so the neighborhood is not disrupted by an increased flow of traffic.

Business Cards are another inexpensive way to inform the public about your business. They are easy to distribute at meetings, the completion of a job, or when networking. Think of your business card as a "mini-billboard". It should contain the name of your business, the name of a contact person, the complete address, the complete phone number, and an appropriate slogan or description of the business.

Promotional Gimmicks are inexpensive give-aways that attract attention. For example, pens inscribed with your logo, balloons with your business name, or t-shirts can be used to promote your product or service.

Radio and Television reach large numbers of people within a geographical area. Charges are calculated by the second of air time, the audience, and the range of the station.

Some guidelines can help you make decisions about how to spend television advertising dollars. Testimonials from satisfied customers, demonstrations of a product, and illustrations of problems solved through the use of your product are all sales techniques that have been successful for television advertisers.

Local radio advertising targets highly specific audiences. Radio advertisements must be used frequently to get results and could prove to be more costly than newspaper ads in the long run.

IN SUMMARY

Pay attention to advertisements that attract your attention. Try to analyze successful advertising done by professionals for tips on designing your own ads. Your advertising should be the highest quality you can afford and as professional as possible. Your advertising represents you and your business and conveys an impression to the public.

All promotion costs something. Advertising is a necessary expense for establishing, maintaining, and expanding your business.

The size of your advertising budget should be determined by long-range as well as immediate sales objectives. Although the proportion of income spent on advertising varies according to the type of business, the average is 1.5%. The Small Business Administration suggests it is not the amount that is spent but how it is spent that counts. The rule of thumb is that the cost of advertising should be offset by the increase in its resulting profits. Advertising must be cost-effective.

Advertising identifies a business with the product or service it offers, builds confidence in the business, creates good will, and increases sales. Advertising cannot make a prosperous business out of one that is offering a poor product or inferior service. Untruthful or misleading statements will destroy consumer confidence.

BUSINESS INCUBATORS

THE HOME-BASED ENTREPRENEUR

BUSINESS INCUBATORS

BUSINESS INCUBATORS

Zoning and licensing restrictions may prevent you from locating your business in your home or your business may have become so successful that you have outgrown the home office setting. A new location entity has entered the business arena in the form of the **business incubator** or **venture center.** It is a concept in which many small businesses share in one facility and in common support activities in order to lower costs. Incubators have been developed in many parts of the United States. It is a place designed to foster the growth of small companies.

In general, business incubators are defined as physical facilities that provide new companies with the support services needed to increase their survival rate during their early years of development. Most start-up companies are long on owner energy and determination, but short on working capital and business know-how.

Incubators offer support to the new business in three ways:

1. **Location** — The facility provides flexible space for a number of companies at a low square footage cost. Space may be allocated for light manufacturing, service, commercial high-tech, consulting, wholesale, retail, non-profit, mail-order, import-export, and research and development businesses.

2. **Support Services** — Shared equipment and services are provided that would otherwise be unavailable or unaffordable for the new business. These may include: telephone answering service, central receptionist, business reference library, FAX machine, photocopying equipment, data and word processing, secretarial and clerical support, Federal Express, United Parcel Service pick-up and delivery, parking, group insurance, trash pick-up, janitorial and maintenance service, utilities, security, small business computer and software program use, notary public, use of conference rooms, and on-site child care facilities.

A "use fee" or reservation system may be in place for the use of some services, but the cost is much less than would be incurred if the business owner had to purchase the equipment or service outside the group setting.

3. **Professional Advice and Consulting** — Most incubators are administered by a Board of Directors whose mission is to help the entrepreneur to succeed. Many provide on-site assistance and consulting in areas such as accounting, business and financial planning, marketing and advertising, loan packaging, legal services, tax information, and sources of funding.

Statistics show that legitimate incubators increase their tenant companies' chances of success between 80 to 93 percent. This compares with a 20% success rate in the general economy. Incubators can significantly cut overhead costs for the start-up business. With many of the business decisions such as type of copier to purchase and type of business insurance to purchase taken care of, the entrepreneur can concentrate on the development of his business. The constant reinforcement through interest and encouragement from staff, Board members, and fellow business owners can provide the new owner with the support group lacking in the home office. Information on facilities in your area is available through the SBA and your State Business Development Agencies.

RESOURCE GUIDE

FEDERAL
STATE
ASSOCIATIONS
BOOKS & PUBLICATIONS
LIBRARY RESOURCES

THE HOME-BASED ENTREPRENEUR

RESOURCE GUIDE

THE SMALL BUSINESS ADMINISTRATION

The U.S. Small Business Administration is an independent federal agency which was created by Congress in 1953 to assist, council, and represent small business. Statistics show that most small business failures are due to poor management. For this reason, the SBA places special emphasis on individual counseling, courses, conferences, workshops, and publications to train the new and existing business owner in all facets of business development with special emphasis on improving the management ability of the owner.

Counseling is provided through the Service Corp. of Retired Executives (SCORE), Small Business Institutes (SBI's), Small Business Development Centers (SBDC's), and numerous professional associations. SBA strives to match the need of a specific business with the expertise available.

Business management training covers such topics as planning, finance, organization, and marketing and is held in cooperation with educational institutions, Chambers of Commerce, and trade associations. Pre-business workshops are held on a regular basis for prospective business owners. Other training programs are conducted that focus on special needs such as rural development, young entrepreneurship, and international trade. The following is a brief summary of what these programs include.

SCORE is a 13,000 person volunteer program with over 750 locations. SCORE helps small businesses solve their operating problems through one-on-one counseling and through a well developed system of workshops and training sessions. SCORE counseling is available at no charge.

Small Business Institutes (SBI's) are organized through the SBA on over 500 university and college campuses. At each SBI, on-site management counseling is provided by senior and graduate students at schools of business administration working with faculty advisors. In addition to counseling individual businesses, schools provide economic development assistance to communities. Students are guided by faculty advisors and SBA development staff and receive academic credit for their work.

Small Business Development Centers (SBDC's) draw their resources from local, state and Federal Government programs, the private sector, and university facilities. They provide managerial and technical help, research studies and other types of specialized assistance. These centers are generally located or headquartered in academic institutions and provide individual counseling and practical training for small business owners.

Publications — Business Development has over 100 business publications which are available for a nominal fee. They address the most important questions asked by prospective and existing business owners. A free copy of **Directory of Business Development Publications** can be obtained by contacting your local SBA office or by calling the Small Business Answer Desk at 1(800)368-5855 (in Washington, D.C., call 653-7561). Publications may be ordered by sending a check made out to "U.S. Small Business Administration" to: SBA, P.O. Box 15434, Fort Worth, TX 76119.

Following is a partial listing of publications which are available:

FM 1 - ABC's Of Borrowing

Some small business people cannot understand why a leading institution refused to lend them money. Others have no trouble getting funds but are surprised to find strings attached to their loans. Learn the fundamentals of borrowing.......$1.00.

FM 5 - A Venture Capital Primer for Small Business

This booklet highlights the venture capital resources available and shows how to develop a proposal for obtaining these funds.......50¢.

FM 7 - Analyze Your Records to Reduce Costs

Cost reduction is not simply slashing any and all expenses. Understand the nature of expenses and how they inter-relate with sales, inventories, and profits. Achieve greater profits through more efficient use of the dollar.......50¢.

FM 8 - Budgeting in a Small Business

Learn how to set up and keep sound financial records. Study how to effectively use journals, ledgers, and charts to increase profits.......50¢.

FM 11 - Breakeven Analysis: A Decision Making Tool

Learn how breakeven analysis enables the manager/owner to make better decisions concerning sales, profits, and costs......$1.00.

MP 1 - Effective Business Communications

Explains the importance of business communications and how they play a valuable role in business success.......50¢.

MP 19 - Small Business Decision Making

Acquaint yourself with the wealth of information available on management approaches and techniques to identify, analyze, and solve business problems.......$1.00.

MP 25 - Selecting the Legal Structure for Your Business

Discusses the various legal structures that a small business can use in setting up its operations. It briefly identifies the types of legal structures and lists the advantages and disadvantages of each.......50¢.

MT 1 - Creative Selling: The Competitive Edge

Explains how to use creative selling techniques to increase profits.......50¢.

MT 2 - Marketing for Small Business: An Overview

Provides an overview of the marketing concept and contains an extensive bibliography of sources covering the subject of marketing.......$1.00.

MT 3 - Is the Independent Sales Agent for You?

Provides guidelines that help the owner/manager of a small company determine whether or not a sales agent is needed and provides pointers on how to choose one.......50¢.

MT 6 - Advertising Media Decisions

Discover how to effectively target your product or service to the proper market. This publication also discusses the different advertising media and how to select and use the best media vehicle for your business.......$1.00.

MT 8 - Research Your Market

Learn what market research is and how you can benefit from it. Introduces inexpensive techniques that small business owners can apply to gather facts about their existing customer base and how to expand it.......$1.00.

MT 9 - Selling by Mail Order

Provides basic information on how to run a successful mail order business. Includes information on product selection, pricing, testing, and writing effective advertisements.......$1.00.

PT 1 - Can You Make Money with Your Idea or Invention?

This publication is a step-by-step guide which shows how you can make money by turning your creative ideas into marketable products. It is a resource for entrepreneurs attempting to establish themselves in the marketplace.......50¢.

OTHER FEDERAL RESOURCES

Bureau of Consumer Protection, Division of Special Statutes, 6th and Pennsylvania Avenue, Washington, D.C. 20580.

Write for information related to your specific business.

Consumer Products and Safety Commission, Bureau of Compliance, 5401 Westbard Avenue, Bethesda, MD 20207.

Request catalog of booklets available on product safety considerations.

Federal Trade Commission, Division of Legal and Public Records, Washington, D.C. 20580.

Request trade practice rules applicable to your business.

Food and Drug Administration, 5600 Fishers Land, Rockville, MD 20857.

Send for requirements governing packaging and labeling of food and food-related products.

National Bureau of Standards, Technical Building B 167, Standard Development Services Section, Washington, D.C. 20234.

Request information on special labeling required for products made of special metals such as gold and silver.

Superintendent of Documents, U.S. Government Printing Office, Washington, D.C. 20402.

Request subject bibliography listing for small or home- based business. There are fees for most publications.

U.S. Department of Commerce, Office of Consumer Affairs, Washington, D.C. 20233.

Offers booklets on product warranties, advertising, packaging, and labeling. Write for catalog.

U.S. Department of Labor, 200 Constitution Avenue, NW, Washington, D.C. 20210.

Request catalog of publications covering small business issues.

STATE RESOURCE GUIDE

The following references include federal agencies with offices in the state and the state agencies and departments which can give you information, literature, and referrals to workshops, consulting, and other resources. The **Small Business Administration** was created by Congress in 1953 with the purpose of helping small business owners with financial assistance, management counseling, and training. The SBA also helps get and direct government procurement contracts for small firms. The SBA conducts many seminars and workshops and publishes excellent literature. The **U.S. Department of Commerce** serves business through its district offices. Its services are mainly export oriented, but officials on the district level are knowledgeable about the business conditions in your region and can advise and direct you regarding additional assistance and information. The **U.S. Department of Labor** is a good resource for tracking business and labor trends. The **Internal Revenue Service** provides you with information of your business tax considerations and publishes informational booklets on a variety of topics. They also provide seminars and workshops. The **U.S. Chamber of Commerce** is the largest volunteer business organization in the world and represents all aspects of business in locations throughout the United States. The following listings are for the regional offices. Also contact the Chamber of Commerce in your community for information on your local level. The **U.S. Occupational Safety and Health Administration** can give you information on dealing with hazardous or toxic materials or wastes in your business. **State Business Development Agencies (SBDI)** provide guidance, programs, and services in business development, procurement assistance, and financial assistance. The **State Department of Revenue** can provide you with information regarding sales tax and the seller's permit.

This list is by no means complete, but is intended to give you a good start in gathering information and becoming educated regarding business issues. Write or telephone the agencies for information and request that your company name be added to their mailing lists.

ALABAMA

Small Business Administration
District Office
2121 Eigth Ave., N., Ste. 200
Birmingham, AL 35203-2398
(205)731-1338

U.S. Department of Commerce
908 S. 20th St., Ste. 200-201
Birmingham, AL 35205
(205)254-1331

U.S. Department of Labor
Birmingham, AL Office
(205)731-1305

Internal Revenue Service (IRS)
1(800)424-1040

U.S. Chamber of Commerce
Southeastern Regional Office
223 Perimeter Cntr. Pkwy., NE
Atlanta, GA 30346
(404)393-0140

U.S. Occupational Safety and
Health Administration
(205)882-7100 (Birmingham)
(205)690-2131 (Mobile)

State Business Development Agency
Alabama Development Office
135 S. Union Street
State Capital
Montgomery, AL 36130
(205)263-0048

State Department of Revenue
(205)261-3257

Chamber of Commerce Executives
Association of Alabama
P.O. Box 972
Jasper, AL 35501
(205)384-4571

ALASKA

Small Business Administration
District Office
701 C Street, Box 67
Anchorage, AK 99513
(907)271-4022

U.S. Department of Commerce
701 C Street, P.O. Box 32
Anchorage, AK 99513
(907)271-5041

U.S. Department of Labor
Through Seattle, WA Office
(206)442-4482

Internal Revenue Service (IRS)
1(800)554-4477

U.S. Chamber of Commerce
Western Regional Office
500 Airport Blvd., Ste. 240
Burlingame, CA 94010
(415)348-4011

U.S. Occupational Safety and
Health Administration
(907)271-5152 (Anchorage)

State Business Development Agency
Office of Enterprise
Dept. of Commerce
Pouch D
Juneau, AK 99811
(907)465-2018

State Department of Revenue
(907)276-2678

Alaska State Chamber of
Commerce
310 Second Street
Juneau, AK 99801
(907)586-2323

ARIZONA

Small Business Administration
District Office
2005 N. Central Ave., 5th Fl.
Pheonix, AZ 85004
(602)261-3732

U.S. Department of Commerce
Valley Bank Center, Ste. 2750
201 N. Central Ave.
Phoenix, AZ 85073
(602)261-3285

U.S. Department of Labor
Phoenix Office
(602)241-2990

Internal Revenue Service
Phoenix 252-4909
Elsewhere 1(800)554-4477

U.S. Chamber of Commerce
Western Regional Office
500 Airport Blvd., Ste. 240
Burlingame, CA 94010
(415)348-4011

U.S. Occupational Safety and
Health Administration
(602)241-2007

State Business Development Agency
Office of Business and Trade
Department of Commerce
1700 W. Washington St., 4th Fl.
Phoenix, AZ 85007
(602)255-5371

State Department of Revenue
(602)255-3381 (Pheonix)

Arizona Chamber of Commerce
1366 E. Thomas Rd., Ste. 202
Phoenix, AZ 85014
(602)248-9172

ARKANSAS

Small Business Administration
District Office
320 W. Capital Ave., Rm. 601
Little Rock, AR 72201
(501)378-5813

U.S. Department of Commerce
Savers Federal Bldg., Ste.635
320 W. Capitol Ave.
Little Rock, AR 72201
(501)378-5794

U.S. Department of Labor
Little Rock Office
(501)378-5292

Internal Revenue Service
1(800)554-4477

U.S. Chamber of Commerce
Southwestern Regional Office
4835 LBJ Freeway, Ste. 750
Dallas, TX 75234
(214)387-0404

U.S. Occupational Safety and
Health Administration
(501)378-6291

State Business Development Agency
Small Business Development Center
University of Arkansas, Little Rock
Library Bldg., Room 512
Little Rock, AR 72204
(501)371-5381

State Department of Revenue
(501)371-1476

Arkansas Chamber of Commerce
P.O. Box 3645
Little Rock, AR 72203-3645
(501)374-9225

CALIFORNIA

Small Business Administration
District Offices

211 Main Street, 4th Floor
San Francisco, CA 94105
(415)974-0590

2202 Monterey Street, Room 108
Fresno, CA 93721
(209)487-5605

350 S. Figueroa Street, 6th Floor
Los Angeles, CA 90071
(213)894-7172

880 Front St., Rm. 4-S-29
San Diego, CA 92188
(619)293-7250

2700 N. Main St., Room 400
Santa Ana, CA 92701
(714)836-2494

Internal Revenue Service
Counties of Amador, Calaveras,
Contra Costa, Marin, and
San Joaquin: 1(800)428-4032
Los Angeles: (213)617-3177
Oakland: (415)839-424
    Elsewhere: 1(800)554-4477

U.S. Department of Commerce
11777 San Vicente Blvd., Rm. 800
Los Angeles, CA 90049
(213)209-6707

U.S. Department of Labor
Sacramento Office
(916)978-4233

U.S. Occupational Safety and Health Administration
(213)514-6387 (Long Beach)

State Business Development Agency
Office of Small Business Development
Department of Commerce
1121 L. St., Ste. 600
Sacramento, CA 95814
(916)445-6545

State Department of Revenue
(State Board of Equalization)
(916)445-6464 (Sacramento)

California Chamber of Commerce
P.O. Box 1736
(916)444-6670

U.S. Chamber of Commerce
Western Regional Office
500 Airport Blvd., Ste. 240
Burlingame, CA 94010
(415)348-4011

COLORADO

Small Business Administration
District Office
721 19th St., Rm. 454
Denver, CO 80202
(303)844-3984

U.S. Department of Commerce
U.S. Customhouse, Rm. 119
721 19th St.
Denver, CO 80202
(303)837-3246

U.S. Department of Labor
Denver Office
(303)844-4405

Internal Revenue Service
Denver: (303)592-1118
Elsewhere: 1(800)554-4477

U.S. Chamber of Commerce
Northwest Regional Office
Southdale Place
3400 W. 66th St., Ste. 300
Minneapolis, MN 55435
(612)925-2400

U.S. Occupational Safety and
Health Administration
(303)844-5285 (Denver)

State Business Development Agency
Business Information Center
Office of Regulatory Reform
1525 Sherman St., Rm. 110
Denver, CO 80203
(303)866-3933

State Department of Revenue
(303)534-1209 (Denver)

Colorado Association of
Commerce and Industry
1860 Lincoln, Ste. 550
Denver, CO 80295-0501
(303)831-7411

CONNECTICUT

Small Business Administration
District Office
One Hartford Square, West
Hartford, CT 06106
(203)722-2544

U.S. Department of Commerce
Federal Office Building, Rm. 610B
450 Main St.
Hartford, CT 06103
(203)244-3530

U.S. Department of Labor
Hartford
(203)722-2660

Internal Revenue Service
1(800)554-4477

U.S. Chamber of Commerce
Northeast Regional Office
711 Third Ave., Ste. 1702
New York, NY 10017
(212)370-1440

U.S. Occupational Safety and
Health Administration
(203)722-2294 (Hartford)

State Business Development Agency
Small Business Service
Dept. of Economic Development
210 Washington St.
Hartford, CT 06106
(203)566-4051

State Department of Revenue
(203)566-8520 (Hartford)

Connecticut Business and
Industry Association
370 Asylum St.
Hartford, CT 06103
(203)547-1661

DELAWARE

Small Business Administration
Branch Office
844 King St., Rm. 5207
Wilmington, DE 19801
(302)573-6295

U.S. Department of Commerce
9448 Federal Building
600 Arch Street
Philadelphia, PA 19106
(215)597-2866

U.S. Department of Labor
Wilmington
(302)573-6112

Internal Revenue Service
1(800)554-4477

U.S. Chamber of Commerce
Northeastern Regional Office
711 Third Ave., Ste. 1702
New York, NY 10017
(212)370-1400

**U.S. Occupational Safety and
   Health Administration**
(302)573-6115

State Business Development Agency
Economic Development Office
99 King's Highway
P.O. Box 1401
Dover, DE 19903
(302)736-4271

State Department of Revenue
(302)571-3300

**Delaware State Chamber of
   Commerce**
One Commerce Center, Ste. 200
Wilmington, DE 29801
(302)655-7221

DISTRICT OF COLUMBIA

Small Business Administration
District Office
1111 18th St., NW, 6th Fl.
Washington, DC 20036
(202)634-6200

U.S. Department of Commerce
415 U.S. Customhouse
Gay and Lombard Sts.
Baltimore, MD 21202
(301)962-3560

U.S. Department of Labor
Hyattsville, MD
(301)436-6776

Internal Revenue Service
488-3100

U.S. Chamber of Commerce
Southeastern Regional Office
223 Perimeter Center Pkwy., NE
Atlanta, GA 30346
(404)393-0140

**U.S. Occupational Safety and
   Health Administration**
(202)523-8151

State Business Development Agency
Office of Business and Economic
   Development
1111 E. St., NW, Ste. 700
Washington, DC 20004
(202)727-6600

State Department of Revenue
(202)629-4665

**District of Columbia Chamber
   of Commerce**
2100 M St., NW, Ste. 607
Washington, DC 20037
(202)296-0335

FLORIDA

Small Business Administration
District Office
400 W. Bay St., Rm. 261
Jacksonville, FL 32202
(904)791-3105

U.S. Department of Commerce
Federal Bldg., Ste. 224
51 SW First Ave.
Miami, FL 33130
(305)350-5267

U.S. Department of Labor
(904)791-2489 (Jacksonville)
(305)527-7262 (Fort Lauderdale)
(813)228-2154 (Tampa)

Internal Revenue Service
Jacksonville: 353-9579
Elsewhere: 1(800)554-4477

U.S. Chamber of Commerce
Southeastern Regional Office
223 Perimeter Center Pkwy., NE
Atlanta, GA 30346
(404)393-0140

**U.S. Occupational Safety and
    Health Administration**
(813)228-2821 (Tampa)
(305)527-7292 (Fort Lauderdale)

State Business Development Agency
Small Business Development Center
University of West Florida, Bldg. 8
Pensacola, FL 32514
(904)474-2908

State Department of Revenue
(904)488-2574

**Central Florida Small Business
    Association**
P.O. Box 30533
Orlando, FL 32862
(305)859-5013

GEORGIA

Small Business Administration
District Office
1720 Peachtree Rd., NW, 6th Fl.
Atlanta, GA 30309
(404)347-2441

U.S. Department of Commerce
1365 Peachtree Rd., NE, Ste. 600
Atlanta, GA 30309
(404)881-7000

U.S. Department of Labor
(404)347-4801 (Atlanta)
(912)944-4222 (Savannah)

Internal Revenue Service
Atlanta: 522-0050
Elsewhere: 1(800)424-1040

U.S. Chamber of Commerce
Southeastern Regional Office
223 Perimeter Center Pkwy., NE
Atlanta, GA 30346
(404)393-0140

**U.S. Occupational Safety and
    Health Administration**
(404)331-4767 (Tucker)
(912)233-3923 (Savannah)

State Business Development Agency
Small Business Development Center
1180 E. Broad St., Chicopee Complex
Athens, GA 30602
(404)542-1721

State Department of Revenue
(404)656-4015

Business Council of Georgia
1280 S. Omni International
Atlanta, GA 30335
(404)223-2264

HAWAII

Small Business Administration
District Office
300 Ala Moana, Rm. 2213
Honolulu, HI 96813
(808)546-3119

U.S. Department of Commerce
4106 Federal Bldg.
P.O. Box 50026
300 Ala Moana Blvd.
Honolulu, HI 96813
(808)546-8694

U.S Department of Labor
(808)546-8363

Internal Revenue Service
Oahu: 541-1040
Elsewhere: 1(800)424-1040

U.S. Chamber of Commerce
Western Regional Office
500 Airport Blvd., Ste. 240
Burlingame, CA 94010
(415)348-4011

**U.S. Occupational Safety and
    Health Administration**
(808)546-3157

State Business Development Agency
Small Business Information Service
250 S. King St., Rm. 724
Honolulu, HI 96813
(808)548-7650

State Department of Taxation
(808)548-7650

Hawaii Chamber of Commerce
Dillingham Building
735 Bishop St.
Honolulu, HI 96813
1(808)531-4111

IDAHO

Small Business Administration
District Office
1020 Main St., Ste. 290
Boise, ID 83702
(208)334-1780

U.S. Department of Commerce
Statehouse
Boise, ID 83702
(208)334-2470

U.S. Department of Labor
(208)334-1029

Internal Revenue Service
1(800)554-4477

U.S. Chamber of Commerce
Western Regional Office
500 Airport Blvd., Ste. 240
Burlingame, CA 94010
(415)348-4011

**U.S. Occupational Safety and
    Health Administration**
(208)334-1867

State Business Development Agency
Division of Economic & Community Affairs
Dept. of Commerce, State Capitol, Rm. 108
Boise, ID 83702
(202)334-2470

State Department of Revenue
(208)334-3560

**Idaho Association of Commerce
    and Industry**
P.O. Box 389
Boise, ID 8370
(208)343-1849

ILLINOIS

Small Business Administration
District Office
219 S. Dearborn St., Rm. 437
Chicago, IL 60604
(312)353-7723

U.S. Department of Commerce
1406 Mid Continental Plaza Bldg.
55 E. Monroe St.
Chicago, IL 60603
(312)353-4450

U.S. Department of Labor
(312)353-8145

Internal Revenue Service
Chicago: 435-1040
Elsewhere: 1(800)424-1040

U.S. Chamber of Commerce
North Central Region
1200 Harger Rd., Ste. 606
Oak Brook, IL 60521
(312)325-7818

**U.S. Occupational Safety and
    Health Administration**
(312)891-3800

State Business Development Agency
Bureau of Small Business
Department of Commerce and
    Community Affairs
620 E. Adams St.
Springfield, IL 62701
(217)785-7500

State Department of Revenue
(217)782-3336 (Springfield)

**Illinois State Chamber of
 Commerce**
215 E. Adams St.
Springfield, IL 62701
(217)522-5512

INDIANA

Small Business Administration
District Office
575 N. Pennsylvania St., Rm. 578
Indianapolis, IN 46204
(317)269-7264

U.S. Department of Commerce
357 U.S. Courthouse & Federal Bldg.
46 E. Ohio St.
Indianapolis, IN 46204
(317)269-6214

U.S. Department of Labor
(317)232-2680

Internal Revenue Service
Indianapolis: 226-5477
Elsewhere:1(800)424-1040

U.S. Chamber of Commerce
North Central Region
1200 Harger Rd., Ste. 606
Oak Brook, IL 60521
(312)325-7818

**U.S. Occupational Safety and
    Health Administration**
(317)269-7290

State Business Development Agency
Division of Small Business
    Expansion
Department of Commerce
1 N. Capital Ave., Ste. 700
Indianapolis, IN 46204
(317)232-8800

State Department of Revenue
(317)232-2330

**Indiana State Chamber of
    Commerce**
1 N. Capitol Ave., Ste. 200
Indianapolis, IN 46204
(317)634-6407

IOWA

Small Business Administration
District Offices

373 Collins Rd., NE
Cedar Rapids, IA 52402
(319)399-2571

210 Walnut St., Rm. 749
Des Moines, IA 50309
(515)284-4760

U.S. Department of Commerce
817 Federal Building
210 Walnut St.
Des Moines, IA 50309
(515)284-4222

U.S. Department of Labor
(515)284-4624

Internal Revenue Service
Des Moines: 283-0523
Elsewhere: 1(800)424-1040

U.S. Chamber of Commerce
Northwestern Regional Office
Southdale Place
3400 W. 66th St., Ste. 300
Minneapolis, MN 55435
(612)925-2400

**U.S. Occupational Safety and
Health Administration**
(515)284-4794

State Business Development Agency
Small Business Section
Iowa Development Commission
200 E. Grand Ave.
Des Moines, IA 50309
(515)281-8310

State Department of Revenue
(515)281-3114

Iowa Development Commission
600 E. Court Ave.
Des Moines, IA 50309
1(800)532-1216

KANSAS

Small Business Administration
District Offices

11- E. Waterman St.
Wichita, KS 67202
(316)269-6273

1103 Grande Ave., Rm. 512
Kansas City, MO 64106
(816)374-5868

U.S. Department of Commerce
P.O. Box 48
Wichita State University
Wichita, KS 67208
(316)269-6160

U.S. Department of Labor
(816)374-5721

Internal Revenue Service
1(800)424-1040

U.S. Chamber of Commerce
Northwestern Regional Office
Southdale Place
3400 W. 66th St., Ste. 300
Minneapolis, MN 55435
(615)925-2400

**U.S. Occupational Safety and
Health Administration**
(316)269-6644

State Business Development Agency
Small Business Development Center
Wichita State University
021 Clinton Hall, Campus Box 148
Wichita, KS 67208
(316)689-3193

State Department of Revenue
(913)296-3909

**Kansas Chamber of Commerce
and Industry**
500 Bank IV Tower
Topeka, KS 66603
(913)357-6321

KENTUCKY

Small Business Administration
District Office
600 Federal Place, Rm. 188
Louisville, KY 40201
(502)582-5976

U.S. Department of Commerce
U.S. Post Office & Courthouse
    Building, Rm. 636B
Louisville, KY 40202
(502)582-5066

U.S. Department of Labor
(502)582-5226

Internal Revenue Service
1(800)424-1040

U.S. Chamber of Commerce
North Central Regional Office
1200 Harger Rd., Ste. 606
Oak Brook, IL 60521
(312)325-7818

U.S. Occupational Safety and
    Health Administration
(502)277-7024

State Business Development Agency
Business Information Clearinghouse
Commerce Cabinet
Capitol Plaza Tower, 22nd Fl.
Frankfort, KY 40601
(502)564-4252
    (504)342-5361

State Department of Revenue
(502)564-8054

Kentucky Chamber of Commerce
P.O. Box 817
Frankfort, KY 40602
(502)695-4700

LOUISIANA

Small Business Administration
District Office
1661 Canal St., Ste. 2000
New Orleans, LA 70112
(504)589-2354

U.S. Department of Commerce
432 International Trade Mart
No. 2 Canal St.
New Orleans, LA 70130
(504)589-6546

U.S. Department of Labor
(504)589-6171

Internal Revenue Service
1(800)424-1040

U.S. Chamber of Commerce
Southwest Regional Office
4835 LBJ Freeway, Ste. 750
Dallas, TX 75234
(214)387-0404

U.S. Occupational Safety and
    Health Administration
(504)389-0474

State Business Development Agency
Department of Commerce
Office of Commerce and Industry
One Maritime Plaza
P.O. Box 94185
Baton Rouge, LA 70802

State Department of Revenue
(504)568-5233

Louisiana Association of Business
    and Industry
P.O. Box 80258
Baton Rouge, LA 70898
    (504)928-5388

MAINE

Small Business Administration
District Office
40 Western Ave., Rm. 512
Augusta, ME 04330
(207)622-8242

U.S. Department of Commerce
Casco Bank Building
1 Memorial Circle
Augusta, ME 04330
(207)622-8249

U.S. Department of Labor
(207)780-3344 (Portland)

Internal Revenue Service
1(800)424-1040

U.S. Chamber of Commerce
Northeastern Regional Office
711 Third Ave., Ste. 1702
New York, NY 10017
(212)370-1440

**U.S. Occupational Safety and
Health Administration**
(207)622-8417

State Business Development Agency
Small Business Development Center
University of Southern Maine
246 Deering Ave.
Portland, ME 04102
(207)780-4420

State Tax Commission
(207)289-3695

**Maine Chamber of Commerce
and Industry**
126 Sewall St.
Augusta, ME 04330
(207)623-4568

MARYLAND

Small Business Administration
District Office
10 N. Calvert St.
Equitable Bldg., 3rd Fl.
Baltimore, MD 21202
(301)962-2233

U.S. Department of Commerce
415 U.S. Customhouse
Gay & Lombard Sts.
Baltimore, MD 21202
(301)962-3560

U.S. Department of Labor
(301)962-2265

Internal Revenue Service
Baltimore: 962-2590
Montgomery Co.: 488-3100
Prince George Co.: 488-3100
Elsewhere: 1(800)424-1040

U.S. Chamber of Commerce
Southeastern Regional Office
223 Perimeter Center Pkwy., NE
Atlanta, GA 30346
(404)393-0140

**U.S. Occupational Safety and
Health Administration**
(301)962-2840

State Business Development Agency
Office of Business & Industrial
Development
45 Calvert St.
Annapolis, MD 21404
(301)269-2945

State Department of Revenue
(301)225-1350

Maryland Chamber of Commerce
60 West St.
Annapolis, MD 21401
(301)261-2858

MASSACHUSETTS

Small Business Administration
District Office
150 Causeway St., 10th Fl.
Boston, MA 02114
(617)223-7991

U.S. Department of Commerce
441 Stuart St., 10th Fl.
Boston, MA 02116
(617)223-2312
   (313)226-3650

U.S. Department of Labor
(617)223-6751

Internal Revenue Service
Boston: 523-1040
Elsewhere: 1(800)424-1040

U.S. Chamber of Commerce
Northeastern Regional Office
711 Third Ave.,Ste. 1702
New York, NY 10017
   (312)325-7818

U.S. Occupational Safety amd
   Health Administration
(617)647-8681 (Waltham)
(413)785-0123 (Springfield)

State Business Development Agency
Small Business Assistance Division
Department of Commerce
100 Cambridge St., 13th Fl.
Boston, MA 02202
(617)727-4005

State Department of Revenue
(617)727-4393

Smaller Business Association
   of New England
69 Hickory Drive
Waltham, MA 02154
(617)890-9070

MICHIGAN

Small Business Administration
District Office
477 Michigan Ave., Rm. 515
Detroit, MI 48226
(313)226-6075

U.S. Department of Commerce
445 Federal Building
231 W. Lafayette
Detroit, MI 48226

U.S. Department of Labor
(616)456-2333 (Grand Rapids)

Internal Revenue Service
Detroit:237-0800
Elsewhere: 1(800)424-1040

U.S. Chamber of Commerce
North Central Regional Office
1200 Harger Rd., Ste. 606
Oak Brook, IL 60521

U.S. Occupational Safety and
   Health Administration
(517)322-1851

State Business Development Agency
Local Development Service
Department of Commerce
P.O. Box 30225
Lansing, MI 48908
(517)373-3530

State Department of Revenue
(517)373-9626

Michigan State Chamber
   of Commerce
Business and Trade Center, Ste. 400
200 N. Washington Square
Lansing, MI 48933
   (517)485-3409

MINNESOTA

Small Business Administration
District Office
100 N. Sixth St., Ste. 610
Minneapolis, MN 55403
(612)349-3574

U.S. Department of Commerce
108 Federal Building
110 S. Fourth St.
Minneapolis, MN 55401
(612)349-3338

U.S. Department of Labor
(612)349-3701

Internal Revenue Service
Minneapolis: 291-1422
St. Paul: 291-1422
Elsewhere: 1(800)424-1040

U.S. Chamber of Commerce
Northwestern Regional Office
Southdale Place
3400 W. 66th St., Ste. 300
Minneapolis, MN 55435

**U.S. Occupational Safety and
   Health Administration**
(612)349-5994

State Business Development Agency
Small Business Assistance Division
Dept. of Energy & Economic Development
900 American Center
150 E. Kellogg Blvd.
St. Paul, MN 55107
(612)296-3871

State Department of Revenue
(612)642-0372

**Minnesota Association of Commerce
   and Industry**
300 Hanover Building
480 Cedar St.
St. Paul, MN 55101
(612)292-4650

MISSISSIPPI

Small Business Administration
District Office
100 W. Capitol St., Ste. 322
Jackson, MS 36269
(601)965-5332

U.S. Department of Commerce
Jackson Mall Office Center, Ste. 3230
300 Woodrow Wilson Blvd.
Jackson, MS 39213
(601)960-4388

U.S. Department of Labor
(601)965-4347

Internal Revenue Service
1(800)424-1040

U.S. Chamber of Commerce
Southeastern Regional Office
223 Perimeter Center Pkwy., NE
Atlanta, GA 30346
(404)393-0140

**U.S. Occupational Safety and
   Health Administration**
(601)965-4606

State Business Development Agency
Small Business Clearinghouse
Research & Development Center
3825 Ridgewood Rd.
Jackson, MS 39211
(601)982-6231

State Department of Revenue
(601)359-1141

Department of Economic Development
P.O. Box 849
Jackson, MS 39205
(601)359-3437

MISSOURI

Small Business Administration
District Offices

1103 Grande Ave., Room 512
Kansas City, MO 64106
(816)374-5868

815 Olive Street
St. Louis, MO 63101
(314)425-6600

U.S. Department of Commerce
120 S. Central Avenue
St. Louis, MO 63105
(314)425-3302

U.S. Department of Labor
(314)425-4706 (St. Louis)
(816)374-5721 (Kansas City)

Internal Revenue Service
St. Louis: 342-1040
Elsewhere: 1(800)424-1040

U.S. Chamber of Commerce
Southwestern Regional Office
4835 LBJ Freeway, Suite 750
Dallas, TX 75234
(214)387-0404

**U.S. Occupational Safety and
    Health Administration**
(816)374-2756
(314)263-2749

State Business Development Agency
Small & Existing Business Development
    Office
Department of Economic Development
P.O. Box 118
Jefferson City, MO 65102
(314)751-4982

State Department of Revenue
(314)751-2151

MONTANA

Small Business Administration
District Office
    301 S. Park, Room 528
Helena, MT 59626
(406)449-5381

U.S. Department of Commerce
U.S. Customhouse, Room 119
721 19th Street
Denver, CO 80202
(303)837-3246

U.S. Department of Labor
(801)424-1040

Internal Revenue Service
1(800)424-1040

U.S. Chamber of Commerce
Northwestern Regional Office
Southdale Place
3400 W. 66th Street, Suite 300
Minneapolis, MN 55435

**U.S. Occupational Safety and
    Health Administration**
(406)657-6649 (Billings)

State Business Development Agency
Business Assistance Division
Department of Commerce
1424 Ninth Avenue
Helena, MT 59620
(406)444-3923

State Department of Revenue
(406)444-2460

MISSOURI (Con't)

Missouri Chamber of Commerce
Missouri Center for Free Enterprise
P.O. Box 149
428 E. Capitol Avenue
Jefferson City, MO 65102
(314)634-3616

NEBRASKA

Small Business Administration
District Office
11145 Mill Valley Road
Omaha, NE 68154
(402)221-3604

U.S. Department of Commerce
Empire State Building, 1st Fl.
300 S. 19th St.
Omaha, NE 68102
(402)221-3664

U.S. Department of Labor
(402)221-4682

Internal Revenue Service
Omaha: 422-1500
Elsewhere: 1(800)424-1040

U.S. Chamber of Commerce
Northwestern Regional Office
Southdale Place
3400 W. 66th St., Ste. 300
Minneapolis, MN 55435
(612)925-2400

U.S. Occupational Safety and
   Health Administration
(402)221-3182

State Business Development Agency
Small Business Division
Dept. of Economic Development
P.O. Box 94666
301 Centennial Mall South
Lincoln, NE 68509
(402)471-3111

State Department of Revenue
(402)471-2971

MONTANA (Con't)

Montana Chamber of Commerce
P.O. Box 1730
Helena, MT 59624
(406)442-2405

NEVADA

Small Business Administration
District Office
301 E. Stewart St.
Las Vegas, NV 89125
(702)388-6611

U.S. Department of Commerce
1755 E. Plumb Ln., #152
Reno, NV 89502
(702)784-5203

U.S. Department of Labor
(702)784-5200

Internal Revenue Service
1(800)424-1040

U.S. Chamber of Commerce
Western Regional Office
500 Airport Blvd., Ste. 240
Burlingame, CA 94010
(415)348-4011

U.S. Occupational Safety and
   Health Administration
(702)388-6163 (Las Vegas)

State Business Development Agency
Small Business Development Center
University of Nevada (Reno)
College of Business Administration
Business Bldg., Rm. 411
Reno, NV 89557
(702)784-1717

State Department of Taxation
(702)885-4820

NEBRASKA (Con't)

**Nebraska Association of Commerce
    and Industry**
P.O. Box 95128
1320 Lincoln Mall
Lincoln, NE 68509
(402)474-5255

NEVADA (Con't)

Commission of Economic Development
Capital Complex
Carson City, NV 89701
(702)885-4325

NEW HAMPSHIRE

Small Business Administration
District Office
55 Pleasant St., Rm. 211
Concord, NH 03301
(603)225-1400

U.S. Department of Commerce
411 Stuart St., 4th Fl.
Boston, MA 02116
(617)223-2312

U.S. Department of Labor
(207)780-3344 (Portland, ME)

Internal Revenue Service
1(800)424-1040

U.S. Chamber of Commerce
Northeastern Regional Office
711 Third Ave., Ste. 1702
New York, NY 10017
(212)370-1440

**U.S. Occupational Safety and
    Health Administration**
(603)225-1629 (Concord)

State Business Development Agency
Industrial Development Authority
4 Park St., Rm. 302
Concord, NH 03301
(603)2781-2591

NEW JERSEY

Small Business Administration
District Office
60 Park Place, 4th Fl.
Newark, NJ 07102
(201)645-2434

U.S. Department of Commerce
Capitol Plaza, 8th Fl.
240 W. State St.
Trenton, NJ 08608
(609)989-2100

U.S. Department of Labor
(201)645-2279 (Newark)
(609)989-2247 (Trenton)

Internal Revenue Service
Newark: 622-0600
Elsewhere: 1(800)424-1040

U.S. Chamber of Commerce
Northeastern Regional Office
711 Third Ave., Ste. 1702
New York, NY 10017
(212)370-1440

**U.S. Occupational Safety and
    Health Administration**
(609)757-5181 (Camden)
(201)361-4050 (Dover)

State Business Development Agency
Office of Small Business Assistance
Dept. of Commerce & Economic Development
1 W. State St., CN 823
Trenton, NJ 08625
(609)984-4442

NEW HAMPSHIRE (Con't)

State Department of Revenue
(603)271-2191

New England Business Association
P.O. Box 535
Plaistow, NH 03856
(603)382-4711

NEW JERSEY (Con't)

State Department of Revenue
(609)292-7592

**New Jersey State Chamber
of Commerce**
5 Commerce St.
Newark, NJ 07102
(201)622-7690

NEW MEXICO

Small Business Administration
District Office
5000 Marble Ave., NE, Rm. 320
Albuquerque, NM 87100
(505)766-3588

U.S. Department of Commerce
505 Marquette Ave., NW, Ste. 1015
Albuquerque, NM 87102
(505)766-2386

U.S. Department of Labor
(505)766-2477

Internal Revenue Service
1(800)424-1040

NEW YORK

Small Business Administration
District Office

26 Federal Plaza, Rm. 3100
New York, NY 10278
(212)264-1480

100 S. Clinton St., Rm. 1071
Syracuse, NY 13260
(315)423-5376

U.S. Department of Commerce
1312 Federal Building
111 W. Huron St.
Buffalo, NY 14202
(716)846-4191

Federal Office Building
26 Federal Plaza - Foley Square
New York, NY 10278
(212)264-0634

U.S. Department of Labor
(212)264-8185 (New York City)
(518)472-3596 (Albany)

Internal Revenue Service
Bronx: 732-0100
Brooklyn: 596-3700
Buffalo: 855-3955
Manhattan: 732-0100
Nassau: 222-1131
Queens: 596-3770
Rockland Co.: 997-1510
Elsewhere: 1(800)424-1040

NEW MEXICO (Con't)

U.S. Chamber of Commerce
Southwestern Regional Office
4835 LBJ Freeway, Ste. 750
Dallas, TX 75234
(214)387-0404

**U.S. Occupational Safety and
   Health Administration**
(505)766-3411

State Business Development Agency
Dept. of Economic Development
Joseph Montoya Building
1100 St. Francis Drive
Santa Fe, NM 87503
(505)827-0300

State Department of Revenue
(505)988-2290

**Association of Commerce and
   Industry of New Mexico**
117 Quincy, NE
Albuquerque, NM 87108

NEW YORK (Con't)

U.S. Chamber of Commerce
Northeastern Regional Office
711 Third Ave., Ste. 1702
New York, NY 10017
(212)370-1440

**U.S. Occupational Safety and
   Health Administration**
   (212)264-9840 (New York City)

State Business Development Agency
Small Business Division
Department of Commerce
230 Park Ave., Rm. 834
New York, NY 10169
(212)309-0400

State Department of Revenue
(518)457-7177 (Albany)
  1(800)342-3536 (Tax kit)

Business Council of New York State
152 Washington Ave.
Albany, NY 12210
(518)465-7511

NORTH CAROLINA

Small Business Administration
District Office
230 S. Tryon St., Rm. 700
Charlotte, NC 28202
(704)371-6563

U.S. Department of Commerce
203 Federal Building
W. Market St.
P.O. Box 1950
Greensboro, NC 27402
(919)755-4687

U.S. Department of Labor
(704)371-6120

NORTH DAKOTA

Small Business Administration
District Office
657 Second Ave., North Rm. 218
Fargo, ND 58108
(701)237-5771

U.S. Department of Commerce
Empire State Building, 1st Fl.
300 S. 19th St.
Omaha, NE 68102
(402)221-3664

U.S. Department of Labor
(303)844-4405 (Denver, CO)

NORTH CAROLINA (Con't)

Internal Revenue Service
1(800)424-1040

U.S. Chamber of Commerce
Southeastern Regional Office
223 Perimeter Center Pkwy., NE
Atlanta, GA 30346
(404)393-0140

U.S. Occupational Safety and
Health Administration
(919)733-7166

State Business Development Agency
Small Business Development Division
Department of Commerce
Dobbs Building, Rm. 282
430 N. Salisbury St.
Raleigh, NC 27611
(919)733-6254

State Department of Revenue
(919)829-4682

Department of Community Colleges
Small Business & Business Occupations
20 Education Building
Raleigh, NC 27603
(919)733-6385

NORTH DAKOTA (Con't)

Internal Revenue Service
1(800)424-1040

U.S. Chamber of Commerce
Northwestern Regional Office
Southdale Place
3400 W. 66th, Ste.300
Minneapolis, MN 55435
(612)925-2400

U.S. Occupational Safety and
Health Administration
(701)255-4011

State Business Development Agency
Small Business Specialist
Economic Development Commission
Liberty Memorial Building
Bismark, ND 58505
(701)224-2810

State Department of Revenue
(614)466-7910

North Dakota Chamber of Commerce
P.O. Box 2467
Fargo, ND 58108
(701)237-9461

OHIO

Small Business Administration
District Offices

1240 E. Ninth St., Rm. 317
Cleveland, OH 44199
(216)522-4195

85 Marconi Blvd.
Columbus, OH 43215
(614)469-5548

OKLAHOMA

Small Business Administration
District Office
200 NW Fifth St., Ste. 670
Oklahoma City, OK 73102
(405)231-4491

The Home-Based Entrepreneur

OHIO (Con't)

U.S. Department of Commerce
9504 Federal Office Bldg.
550 Main St.
Cincinnati, OH 45202
(513)684-2944

U.S. Department of Labor
(513)684-2942

Internal Revenue Service
Cincinnati: 621-6281
Cleveland: 522-3000
Elsewhere: 1(800)424-1040

U.S. Chamber of Commerce
North Central Region
1200 Harger Rd., Ste. 606
Oak Brook, IL 60521
(312)325-7818

**U.S. Occupational Safety and
Health Administration**
(216)522-3818

State Business Development Agency
Small Business Office
Department of Development
P.O. Box 1001
Columbus, OH 43266
(614)466-4945

State Department of Revenue
(614)466-7910

Ohio Chamber of Commerce
35 E. Gay St., 2nd Fl.
Columbus, OH 43215
(614)228-4201
(614)228-4201

OREGON

Small Business Administration
District Office
1220 SW Third Ave., Rm. 676
Portland, OR 97204
(503)221-2682

OKLAHOMA(Con't)

U.S. Department of Commerce
4024 Lincoln Blvd.
Oklahoma City, OK 73105
(405)231-5302

U.S. Department of Labor
(918)581-7695

Internal Revenue Service
1(800)424-1040

U.S. Chamber of Commerce
Southwestern Regional Office
4835 LBJ Freeway, Ste. 750
Dallas, TX 75234
(214)387-0404

**U.S. Occupational Safety and
Health Administration**
(405)231-5351

State Business Development Agency
Small Business Development Center
Station A
517 W. University
Durant, OK 74701
(405)924-0277

State Department of Revenue
(405)521-4321

**Oklahoma State Chamber
of Commerce**
4020 N. Lincoln Blvd.
Oklahoma City, OK 73105
(405)424-4003

PENNSYLVANIA

Small Business Administration
District Office
960 Penn Ave., 5th Fl.
Pittsburgh, PA 15222
(412)644-5441

OREGON (Con't)

U.S. Department of Commerce
1220 SW Third Ave., Rm. 618
Portland, OR 97204
(503)221-3001

U.S. Department of Labor
(503)221-3057

Internal Revenue Service
Portland: 221-3960
Elsewhere: 1(800)424-1040

U.S. Chamber of Commerce
Western Regional Office
500 Airport Blvd., Ste. 240
Burlingame, CA 94010
(415)348-4011

**U.S. Occupational Safety and
Health Administration**
(503)221-2252

State Business Development Agency
Economic Development Department
Lane Community College
400 E. 30th Ave.
Eugene, OR 97405
(503)373-1205

Department of Revenue
(503)378-3184

Oregon's Small Business Council
P.O. Box 455
Salem, OR 97308
(503)585-5846

PENNSYLVANIA (Con't)

U.S. Department of Commerce
9448 Federal Building
600 Arch St.
Philadelphia, PA 19106
        (215)597-2866

2002 Federal Building
1000 Liberty Ave.
Pittsburg, PA 1522
(412)644-2850

U.S. Department of Labor
(412)644-2996

Internal Revenue Service
Philadelphia: 574-9900
Pittsburg: 281-0112
Elsewhere: 1(800)424-1040

U.S. Chamber of Commerce
Northeastern Regional Office
711 Third Ave., Ste. 1702
New York, NY 10017
        (212)370-1440

**U.S. Occupational Safety and
Health Administration**
(215)597-4955

State Business Development Agency
Small Business Action Center
Department of Commerce
483 Forum Building
Harrisburg, PA 17120
(717)783-5700

Department of Revenue
(717)787-8201

Pennsylvania Chamber of Commerce
222 N. Third St.
Harrisburg, PA 17101
(717)255-3252

RHODE ISLAND

Small Business Administration
District Office
380 Westminster Mall
Providence, RI 02903
(401)528-4583

U.S. Department of Commerce
7 Jackson Walkway
Providence, RI 02903
(401)277-2605
    (803)765-5345

U.S. Department of Labor
(401)528-5141

Internal Revenue Service
1(800)424-1040

U.S. Chamber of Commerce
Northeastern Regional Office
711 Third Ave., Ste. 1702
New York, NY 10017
(212)370-1440

**U.S. Occupational Safety and
    Health Administration**
(401)528-4669

State Business Development Agency
Small Business Development Division
Department of Economic Development
7 Jackson Walkway
Providence, RI 02903
(401)277-2601

State Department of Revenue
(401)277-2934

**National Federation of Independent
    Business**
159 Elmgrove Ave.
Providence, RI 02906
(401)421-0483

SOUTH CAROLINA

Small Business Administration
District Office
1835 Assembly, 3rd Fl.
Columbia, SC 29201
(803)765-5132

U.S. Department of Commerce
Strom Thurmond Federal Bldg., Ste. 172
1835 Assembly St.
Columbia, SC 29201

U.S. Department of Labor
(803)765-5981

Internal Revenue Service
1(800)424-1040

U.S. Chamber of Commerce
Southeastern Regional Office
223 Perimeter Center Pkwy., NE
Atlanta, GA 30346
(404)393-0140

**U.S. Occupational Safety and
    Health Administration**
(803)765-5904

State Business Development Agency
Business Assisitance Services &
    Information Center
State Development Board
P.O. Box 927
Columbia, SC 29202

State Department of Revenue
(803)734-0374

**South Carolina Chamber
    of Commerce**
P.O. Box 11278
Columbia, SC 29211
(803)799-4601

SOUTH DAKOTA

Small Business Administration
District Office
101 S. Main Ave., Ste. 101
Sioux Falls, SD 57102
(605)330-4231

U.S. Department of Commerce
Empire State Building, 1st Fl.
300 S. 19th St.
Omaha, NE 68102
(402)221-3664

U.S. Department of Labor
(303)844-4405

Internal Revenue Service
1(800)424-1040

U.S. Chamber of Commerce
Northwestern Regional Office
Southdale Place
3400 W. 66th St., Ste. 300
Minneapolis, MN 55435
(612)925-2400

U.S. Occupational Safety and
  Health Administration
(701)255-6690 (N. Dakota Office)

State Business Develpoment Agency
Small Business Development Center
University of South Dakota
414 E. Clark St.
Vermillion, SD 57069
(605)677-5272
    (615)741-2626

State Department of Revenue
(605)339-6672

South Dakota Industry and
  Association of Commerce
P.O. Box 190
Pierre, SD 57501
(605)224-6161

TENNESSEE

Small Business Administration
District Office
404 James Robertson Pkwy., Ste. 1012
Nashville, TN 37219
(615)736-5881

U.S. Department of Commerce
One Commerce Plaza, Ste. 1427
Nashville, TN 37239
(615)251-5161

U.S. Department of Labor
(615)736-5452

Internal Revenue Service
Nashville: 259-4601
Elsewhere: 1(800)424-1040

U.S. Chamber of Commerce
Southeastern Regional Office
223 Perimeter Center Pkwy., NE
Atlanta, GA 30346
(404)393-0140

U.S. Occupational Safety and
  Health Administration
(615)736-5313

State Business Development Agency
Small Business Office
Department of Economic & Community
    Development
320 Sixth Ave., N., 7th Fl.
Nashville, TN 37219

State Department of Revenue
(615)741-2801

State Chamber of Commerce
161 Fourth Ave., N
Nashville, TN 37219
(615)259-3900

TEXAS

Small Business Administration
District Offices
1100 Commerce St., Rm. 3C36
Dallas, TX 75242
(214)767-0495

10737 Gateway West, Ste. 320
El Paso, TX 79902
(915)541-7560

222 E. Van Buren St., Rm. 500
Harlington, TX 78550
(512)423-8934

2525 Murworth, Rm. 112
Houston, TX 77054
(713)660-4420

1611 Tenth St., Ste. 200
Lubbock, TX 79401
(806)743-7481

U.S. Department of Commerce
1100 Commerce St., Rm. 7A5
Dallas, TX 75242
(214)767-0542

2625 Federal Courthouse Building
515 Rusk St.
Houston, TX 77002
(713)229-2578

U.S. Department of Labor
(214)767-6294 (Dallas)
(512)229-6125 (San Antonio)

Internal Revenue Service
Dallas: 742-2440
Ft. Worth: 263-9229
Houston:965-0440
Elsewhere: 1(800)424-1040

U.S. Chamber of Commerce
Southwestern Regional Office
4835 LBJ Freeway, Ste. 750
Dallas, TX 75234
(214)387-0404

**U.S. Occupational Safety and
   Health Administration**
(713)750-1727 (Houston)
(512)482-5783 (Austin)

State Business Development Agency
Small & Minority Business Assistance
Division Economic Development
Commission
P.O. Box 12728, Capitol Station
410 E. Fifth St.
Austin, TX 78711
   (512)472-5059

State Comptroller
(713)227-9940

Texas State Chamber of Commerce
206 W. 13th St., Ste. A
Austin, TX 78701
(512)472-1594

UTAH

Small Business Administration
District Office
125 S. State St., Rm. 2237
Salt Lake City, UT 84138
(801)524-3212

U.S. Department of Commerce
U.S. Courthouse
350 S. Main St.
Salt Lake City, UT 84101
(801)524-5116

U.S. Department of Labor
(801)524-5706

Internal Revenue Service
1(800)424-1040

U.S. Chamber of Commerce
Western Regional Office
500 Airport Blvd., Ste. 240
Burlingame, CA 94010
(415)348-4011

**U.S. Occupational Safety and
   Health Administration**
(801)524-5080

State Business Development Agency
Small Business Development Center
University of Utah
660 S. 200 East, Ste. 418
Salt Lake City, UT 84111
(801)581-7905

State Department of Revenue
(801)328-5111

Utah Council of Small Business
10 S. Main, Ste. 210
Salt Lake City, UT 84101
(801)322-1338

VERMONT

Small Business Administration
District Office
87 State St., Rm. 204
Montpelier, VT 05602
(802)229-9801

U.S. Department of Commerce
441 Stuart St., 10th Fl.
Boston, MA 02116
(617)223-2312

U.S. Department of Labor
(617)223-6751

Internal Revenue Service
1(800)424-1040

U.S. Chamber of Commerce
Northeastern Regional Office
711 Third Ave., Ste. 1702
New York, NY 10017
(212)370-1440

**U.S. Occupational Safety and
   Health Administration**
(603)225-1629

State Business Development Agency
Small Business Development Center
University of Vermont Extension Service
Morrill Hall
Burlington, VT 05405
(802)656-2990

State Department of Revenue
(802)828-2509

Vermont State Chamber of Commerce
P.O. Box 37
Montpelier, VT 05602
(802)229-4619

VIRGINIA

Small Business Administration
District Office
400 N. Eigth St., Rm. 3015
Richmond, VA 23240
(804)771-2410

U.S. Department of Commerce
8010 Federal Building
400 N. Eighth St.
Richmond, VA 23240
(804)771-2246

U.S. Department of Labor
(804)771-2995

Internal Revenue Service
Bailey's Crossing: 557-9230
Richmond: 649-2361
Elsewhere: 1(800)424-1040

U.S. Chamber of Commerce
Southeastern Regional Office
223 Perimeter Center Pkwy., NE
Atlanta, GA 30346
(404)393-0140

**U.S. Occupational Safety and
    Health Administration**
(804)771-2864

State Business Development Agency
Small Business Coordinator
Dept. of Economic Development
1000 Washington Bldg.
Richmond, VA 23219
(804)786-3791

State Department of Revenue
(804)257-8031

Virginia Chamber of Commerce
9 S. Fifth St.
Richmond, VA 23219
(804)644-1607

WASHINGTON

Small Business Administration
District Offices

915 Second Ave., Rm. 1792
Seattle, WA 98174
(206)442-5534

920 W. Riverside Ave., Rm. 651
Spokane, WA 99210
(509)456-5346

U.S. Department of Commerce
Lake Union Building, Rm. 706
1700 Westlake Ave., N.
Seattle, WA 98109
(206)442-5616

U.S. Department of Labor
(206)442-4482

Internal Revenue Service
Seattle: 442-1040
Elsewhere: 1(800)424-1040

U.S. Chamber of Commerce
Western Regional Office
500 Airport Blvd., Ste. 240
Burlingame, CA 94010
(415)348-4011

**U.S. Occupational Safety and
    Health Administration**
(206)442-7520

State Business Development Agency
Small Business Development Center
441 Todd Hall
Washington State University
Pullman, WA 99164
(509)335-1576

State Department Business Services
(206)753-4401 or (206)753-4402

Association of Washington Business
P.O. Box 658
Olympia, WA 95807
(206)943-1600

WEST VIRGINIA

Small Business Administration
District Office
186 W. Main St., 6th Fl.
Clarksburg, WV 26301
(304)623-5631

U.S. Department of Commerce
3000 New Federal Building
500 Quarrier St.
Charleston, WV 25301
(304)343-6181

U.S. Department of Labor
(304)347-5207

Internal Revenue Service
1(800)424-1040

U.S. Chamber of Commerce
Southeastern Regional Office
223 Perimeter Center Pkwy., NE
Atlanta, GA 30346
(404)393-0140
    (612)925-2400

**U.S. Occupational Safety and
    Health Administration**
(304)347-5937

State Business Development Agency
Small Business Division
Governor's Office of Community &
    Industrial Development
Capitol Complex
Charleston, WV 25305
(304)348-2960

State Department of Revenue
1(800)225-5982 (WV calls only)

West Virginia Chamber of Commerce
P.O. Box 2789
Charleston, WV 25330
(304)342-1115

WISCONSIN

Small Business Administration
District Office
212 E. Washington Ave., Rm. 213
Madison, WI 53703
(608)264-5117

U.S. Department of Commerce
Federal Building
U.S. Courthouse
517 E. Wisconsin Ave.
Milwaukee, WI 53202
(414)291-3473

U.S. Department of Labor
(414)291-3585

Internal Revenue Service
Milwaukee: 271-3780
Elsewhere: 1(800)424-1040

U.S. Chamber of Commerce
Northwestern Regional Office
Southdale Place
3400 W. 66th St., Ste. 300
Minneapolis, MN 55435

**U.S. Occupational Safety and
    Health Administration**
(414)291-3315

State Business Development Agency
Small Business Ombudsman
Department of Development
123 W. Washington Ave
P.O. Box 7970
Madison, WI 53707
(608)266-0562

State Department of Revenue
(608)266-1961

**Wisconsin Association of Manufacturers
    and Commerce**
111 E. Wisconsin Ave., Ste. 1600
Milwaukee, WI 53202
    (608)255-2312

WYOMING

Small Business Administration
District Office
100 E. B Street, Rm. 4001
Casper, WY 82602
(307)261-5761

U.S. Department of Commerce
U.S. Customhouse, Rm. 119
721 19th Street
Denver, CO 80202
(303)837-3246

U.S. Department of Labor
(303)844-4405 (Denver Office)

Internal Revenue Service
1(800)424-1040

U.S. Chamber of Commerce
Northwestern Regional Office
Southdale Place
3400 W. 66th St., Ste.300
Minneapolis, MN 55435
(612)925-2400

U.S. Occupational Safety and
    Health Administration
(303)884-5285 (Denver Office)

State Business Development Agency
Economic Development Division
Economic Development & Stabilization
    Board
Herschler Bldg., 3rd Fl. East
Cheyenne, WY 82002
(307)777-7287

State Department of Revenue
(307)777-5287

Greater Cheyenne Chamber of
    Commerce
P.O. Box 1147
Cheyenne, WY 82003
(307)638-3388

ASSOCIATIONS

National Federation of Independent Business, 600 Maryland Avenue, SW, Suite 700, Washington, DC 20024, (202)554-9000.

> The country's largest small business association with more than 500,000 member business owners. In addition to representing small business interests to state and federal governments, it distributes educational information and publications, and holds conferences.

National Association of Small Business Investment Companies (NASBIC), 1156 15th Street NW, Suite 1101, Washington, DC 20005, (202)833-8230.

> Coordinates the activities nationwide of Small Business Investment Companies which are set up to provide financing and management assistance to small businesses. Offers a variety of services to member SBIC's and distributes business publications.

Association of Collegiate Entrepreneurs (ACE), Center for Entrepreneurship, Box 147, Wichita State University, Wichita, KS 67208, (316)689-3000.

> ACE members are student entrepreneurs and the organization holds regional and national conferences, and acts as an information clearing house for young business founders.

National Association for the Self-Employed, (804)232-6273.

> Provides business services to members, including health insurance.

National Business Incubation Association, One President Street, Athens, OH 45701.

> Provides information to members on business incubation, shared services, and publishes NBIA Review.

American Home Business Association, 397 Post Road, Darien, Ct, 06820

> An association which represents the interests of home business. Offers group medical insurance package.

BOOKS AND PUBLICATIONS

Breen, George and A.B. Blankenship, **Do-it-Yourself Marketing Research.** New York, McGraw-Hill, 1982

> Introduces simple and inexpensive marketing research techniques.

Clifford, Denis, and Ralph Warner, **The Partnership Book.** Berkeley, CA, Nolo Press, 1989.

> Covers all the elements involved in forming a partnership. Gives guidelines for writing a partnership agreement and covers new tax rules.

Goldstein, Harvey, **Up Your Cash Flow.** Los Angeles, CA, Granville Publications, 1986. (800)873-7789.

> An easy to read and use business guide for increasing your profits and cash flow.

Hawkin, Paul, **Growing a Business.** New York, Simon and Schuster, 1987.

> Advocates hands-on learning, planning and value-oriented approaches to small business success.

Husch, Tony and Linda Foust, **That's a Great Idea.** Oakland, CA, Gravity Publishing, 1982.

> A well-organized guide with tips for locating markets, as well as evaluating, presenting, and protecting product ideas.

Levinson, Jay Conrad, **Guerilla Marketing: Secrets for Making Big Profits from Your Small Business.** Boston, Houghton-Mifflin, 1984.

> A big help for the small business with a limited marketing budget. Contains creative marketing ideas.

Mancuso, Anthony, **How to Form Your Own California Corporation.** Berkeley, CA, Nolo Press, 1988.

> Although this book deals with forming a corporation in the state of California, it contains valuable information regarding corporate taxation, formation, and organization which would be of interest to any owner choosing this legal structure.

Mancuso, Joseph R., **How to Start, Finance, and Manage Your Own Small Business.** 2nd Edition, Englewood Cliffs, NJ, Prentice-Hall, 1986.

> Contains information both on obtaining start-up financing for small businesses and on raising new money for existing businesses.

Ogilvy, David, **Ogilvy on Advertising.** NY, Crown Publishers, Inc. 1983.

> Considered the "master of contemporary advertising", the author describes lessons learned in over 40 years of doing business, and analyzes changes in the field and future directions.

Pinson, Linda and Jerry Jinnett, **Out of Your Mind...and Into the Marketplace.™** Fullerton, CA, Out of Your Mind Press, 1989.

> A step-by-step guide covering small and home-based start-up from conception of the idea through recordkeeping, marketing, and advertising.

Pinson, Linda and Jerry Jinnett, **Marketing: Researching & Reaching Your Target Market.** Fullerton, CA, Out of Your Mind...and Into the Marketplace, 1989.

> A step-by-step guide for researching the market through examining trends, use of questionnaires, and demographic studies and for reaching the market through trade shows, advertising, publicity. Extensive reference list.

Pinson, Linda and Jerry Jinnett, **Recordkeeping: the Secret to Growth and Profit.** Fullerton, CA, Out of Your Mind...and Into the Marketplace, 1989.

> A "user-friendly" guide for setting up, analyzing, and understanding your business records.

Pinson, Linda and Jerry Jinnette, **Anatomy of a Business Plan.** Fullerton, CA, Out of Your Mind...and Into the Marketplace, 1989.

> A hands-on guide for developing, writing, and using a business plan.

Doing Business In....(various foreign countries). Price Waterhouse Information Guides.

> These free guides provide data on business conditions of countries in which Price Waterhouse works. Separate volumes are available for nearly 100 countries from Antigua to Zimbabwe.

Entrepreneur Magazine, 2392 Morse Avenue, Irvine, CA 92714. (800)352-7449.

> Offers suggestions for improving business operations and articles on entrepreneurs operating profitable small businesses. Monthly columns are devoted to computer updates, financial management tips, and industry trade shows.

INC. Magazine, P.O. Box 2538, Boulder, CO 80322, (617)227-4700.

> Billed as the magazine for growing companies, Inc. contains articles and features of interest to small and growing businesses.

Small Business Reporter, Bank of America, Dept.3120, P.O. Box 37000, San Francisco, CA 94137.

> Series of publications from Bank of America covering business issues such as start-up, company profiles, and financing. Write for catalog.

Venture, the Magazine for Entrepreneurs, 521 Fifth Avenue, New York, NY 10175-0028, (212)682-7373.

> Venture supplies up-to-the-minute developments in new entrepreneur enterprises. Contains features and articles focusing on small business concerns.

LIBRARY RESOURCES

Small Business Source Book. 2nd Edition, Detroit, Gale Research Co. 1988.

> A good starting place for finding consultants, educational institutions, government agencies offering assistance, and publications, as well as specific information sources for over 100 types of popular small businesses.

Encyclopedia of Business Information Sources. 6th Edition, Detroit, Gale Research Co. 1986.

> Lists handbooks, periodicals, directories, trade associations, and more, for over 1200 specific industries and business subjects. Start here in any search for information on your particular type of business.

U.S. Industrial Outlook. Washington, D.C. Industry and Trade Administration, U.S. Department of Commerce, Annual.

> Provides an overview, forecasts and short profiles for 200 American Industries, including both statistics on recent trends and a five-year outlook.

The Small Business Resource Guide. Published for AT&T by Braddock Publications, Washington, D.C., 1985.

> Lists sources of information and assistance from both the public and private sectors to help small businesses solve problems and spot opportunities.

Encyclopedia of Associations.

Lists trade and professional associations throughout the United States. Many publish newsletters and marketing information. These associations can help small business owners stay abreast of the latest industry developments, resolve problems with government or consumers, or get information or assistance with management education.

Reference Book for World Traders. Croner, Ulrich, Queens Village, NY. Croner Publications. Annual with monthly supplements.

This three-volume set lists banks, chambers of commerce, customs, marketing organizations, invoicing procedures, and more, for 185 foreign markets. Sections on export planning, financing, shipping, laws, and tariffs are also included, with a directory of helpful government agencies.

Incubators for Small Business. Office of Private Sector Initiatives, SBA, 1441 L Street NW, Room 317, Washington, DC 20416.

Lists over 170 state government offices and incubators that provide financial and technical aid to new small businesses.

Sourcebook of Franchise Opportunities 1988. Dow-Jones Irwin.

Provides annual directory information for U.S. franchises, and data for investment requirements, royalty and advertising fees, services furnished by the franchiser, projected growth rates, and locations where franchises are licensed to operate.

National Trade and Professional Associations of the United States. Columbia books, Inc., Washington, DC, 1987.

Trade and Professional Associations indexed by association, geographic region, subject and budget.

Gale Directory of Newspapers and Periodicals.

Comprehensive source of print media information.

Bacon's Publicity Checker.

Source of publicity information in the United States.

Standard Periodicals Directory.

Lists periodicals including advertising rates, circulations, publications, broadcast stations, and other media.

BUSINESS RESOURCE LIST

Business Name_____

Address _____

_____

Telephone _____

Owner's Name _____

Legal Structure_____

Date founded _____

City/County Clerk_____

Address _____

_____

Telephone_____

Business License # _____

Renewal Date _____

Zoning Commissioner_____

Address_____

_____

Telephone_____

DBA filing date _____

Newspaper _____

Address _____

Telephone _____

Renewal date_____

Bank_____

Address _____

_____

Telephone _____

Contact Person_____

Account number _____

State Regulatory Agency (sales tax)

Address _____

_____

Telephone _____

Seller's Permit #_____

Date issued_____

Insurance Agent_____

Company _____

Address _____

_____

Telephone_____

Policy # _____

Renewal date _____

Insurance Agent_____

Company_____

Address_____

Telephone_____

Policy Type _____

Renewal date_____

Small Business Administration

Address_____

_____

Telephone_____

Contact person _____

U.S. Department of Commerce

Address_____

_____

Telephone_____

Contact person _____

U.S. Department of Commerce

Address_____

_____

Telephone_____

Contact person _____

Internal Revenue Service

Address_____

_____

Telephone_____

Contact person _____

BUSINESS RESOURCE LIST (Con't)

U.S. Chamber of Commerce
Address_____

_____
Telephone_____
Contact person _____

Local Chamber of Commerce
Address_____

_____
Telephone_____
Contact person _____

U.S. Occupational Health & Safety
Address_____

_____
Telephone_____
Contact person _____

State Business Development Agency
Address_____

_____
Telephone_____
Contact person _____

Business Reference_____
Address_____

_____
Telephone_____
Contact person _____

The Home-Based Entrepreneur

INDEX

A

Accounts payable, 61
    example, 71
Accounts Receivable, 61
    example, 72
Advantages, 13
**ADVANTAGES & DISADVANTAGES
    OF A HOME OFFICE, 11-18**
Advertising. 111, 114
Alabama,128
Alaska, 128
Arizona, 129
Arkansas, 129
Assets, 44, 63
ASSOCIATIONS, 156
Automobile insurance, 92

B

Balance Sheet, 62
    example, 75
Bank account, 37
BOOKS AND PUBLICATIONS, 157
Brochures, 115
Budget, 41
Bureau of Consumer Protection, 126
Business cards, 115
Business forms, 59
BUSINESS INCUBATORS, 117-120
Business license, 10, 35
Business life insurance, 92
Business name, 31
Business planning, 101
BUSINESS VIABILITY, 99-107

C

California, 130
Cartoons, 17, 18
Cash flow, 41
Cash flow statement, 41-53
    example, 51
    form, 53
    instructions, 50, 52
Cash on hand, 42, 46
Cash to be paid out, 42-44
    worksheet, 45
Casualty losses, 91
Chamber of Commerce, 9, 111
    alphabetically by state, 128-155
Checkbook, 62
Child care, 14
Community, 16
Community involvement, 16
Competition, 96
Computer Revolution, 4
Colorado, 131
Connecticut, 131
Consumer Products and
    Safety Commission, 126
Corporation, 34
Cost, 102
Cost of goods sold, 102
"cottage industry", 3
Credibility, 15
Customer records, 61
Customers, 111

D

DBA (doing business as), 36
Day care facility, 80
Deductible mortgage interest, 82
Deductions for business
    use of the home, 80, 81
Delaware, 132
Deliveries, 7
Demographics, 95
Department of Consumer
    Affair, 10
Department of Revenue, 127
    Alphabetically by state, 128-155
Depreciation, 83
Direct expenses, 102
Direct mail, 114
Directories, 115
Disability insurance, 92
Disadvantages, 11
Displays, 113
District of Columbia. 132

E

Employees, 8
Entertainment expense record, 61
    example, 74
Entrepreneurial tests, 21
Environmental Protection Agency, 10
Equity, 47, 62
"exclusive use", 79., 80
Exhibits, 113

F

Fair Labor and Standards
    Act of 1938,   9
FEDERAL RESOURCES, 123
Federal Trade Commission, 126
Fictitious name. 36
Financial advantages, 16
Financial statements, 62-64

F (CON'T)

Files, 59
Fire hazards, 8
Fire insurance, 91
Fixed assets, 61, 70
Flexibility, 13
Florida, 133
Food & Drug Administration, 126
Formula for manufacturers, 105

G

General journal, 59, 60
    example, 66
General records, 61, 65
Georgia, 133

H

Hawaii, 134
Hazardous waste, 8, 10
Health insurance, 92
HISTORY OF HOME-BASED
    BUSINESS, 1-4
Home Office Deduction Limitation, 84
Home maintenance expenses, 81
    direct, 82
    indirect, 82, 83
Hourly rate formula, 116
HOW TO FIND A BUSINESS, 23-28

I

Idaho, 134
Illinois, 135
Impact on family, 15
Income statement, 104
Incubators, 119, 120
Independence, 13
Indiana, 135
Indirect expenses, 102

I (CON'T)

Industrial home work, 9
Industrial Revolution, 3
Industrial Work Act of 1943, 9
INSURANCE CONSIDERATIONS, 89-92
Internal Revenue Service, 87, 127
    alphabetically by state, 128-155
Inventory records, 61
    example, 68. 69
Inventory storage, 8, 80
Iowa, 136
IRS Publications, 87
IS YOUR BUSINESS VIABLE?, 99-107
Isolation, 16

J

Journal, 60

K

Kansas, 136
Kentucky, 137

L

Labor laws, 9
Labor unions, 9
Legal structure, 33-35
Liabilities, 44, 63
Liability insurance, 91
LIBRARY RESOURCES, 159, 160
Licenses, 10
Long-term assets, 44
Louisiana, 137

M

Maine, 138
Manufacturer's Formula, 99

M (CON'T)

Marketing, 138
MARKET RESEARCH, 93-98
Maryland, 138
Massachusetts, 139
Michigan, 139
Minnesota, 140
Mississippi, 140
Missouri, 141
Montana, 141

N

Name, 31
Name availability, 32
National Bureau of Standards, 126
Nebraska, 142
Neighbors, 15
Networking, 113
Nevada, 142
New Hampshire, 143
New Jersey, 143
New Mexico, 144
New York, 144
Newspapers, 114
North Carolina, 145
North Dakota, 146

O

Office supplies, 59
Ohio, 146
Oklahoma, 146
On-site sales, 7
One-Year Projection, 104
Operating expense, 44
Oregon, 147
Owner equity, 44

P

Packaging supplies, 59
Partnership, 34
Pennsylvania, 147
PERSONAL ASSESSMENT, 19-22
Personal liability, 7
Petty cash, 60
Petty Cash Record, 60
    example, 67
Price, 97, 103
Price ceiling, 97
Price floor, 97
Pricing/Costing, 99-107
Profit & Loss Statement, 63
Pro Forma Cash Flow Statement, 48-53
Pro Forma Income Statement, 104
Pro forma statements, 41, 103
**PROMOTING & ADVERTISING A
    HOME-BASED BUSINESS, 109-116**
Promotion, 111
Promotional gimmicks, 115
Property Insurance, 91
Publicity, 112
Public relations, 113

Q

Questionnaires, 95, 96

R

Radio, 115
**RECORDKEEPING FOR A
    HOME-BASED BUSINESS, 55-76**
Recordkeeping schedule, 63-65
Recordkeeping supplies, 59
Rent, 83
Repairs, 83
Resale tax number, 36
RESOURCE GUIDE, 121-162
Rhode Island, 149
Risk taking, 21

S

S Corporation, 35
SBA publications, 124
Sales•Revenues, 46, 47
Sales tax, 36, 37
Salesmanship, 112
SCORE, 123
Security System, 83
Self-employment tax, 104
Seller's permit, 36, 37
Selling expense, 44
Selling price, 103
Signs, 8
Skills, 26
SMALL BUSINESS ADMIN., 123
    Federal level, 127
    State level (alphabetical), 128-155
Small Business Development
    Centers, 124
Small Business Institutes, 123
Sole-proprietorship, 33
Sources of cash, 42-46
    worksheet, 47
South Carolina, 149
South Dakota, 150
Space limitations, 7
Start-up costs, 44
State Business Development Agencies, 127
    Alphabetically by state, 128-155
State Department of Revenue, 127
    Alphabetically by state, 132-159
STATE RESOURCE GUIDE, 128-155
**STEPS TO STARTING A
    BUSINESS, 29-38**
Storage of inventory, 8, 80
Stress, 14
**SUCCESS OR FAILURE: IT DEPENDS
    ON YOUR CASH FLOW, 39-53**
Superintendent of Documents, 126

T

**TAX DEDUCTIONS FOR A
    HOME-BASED BUSINESS, 77-87**

T (CON'T)

Tax information, 87
Tax worksheet, 86
"Telecommute", 4
Television, 115
Tennessee, 150
Texas, 151
Time Allocation, 81
Trade associations, 96
Trade shows, 113
Travel expense, 61
    example, 73
Trends, 96
Types of businesses, 27, 28

U

Unrelated expenses, 84
U.S. Department of Commerce, 127
    Alphabetically by state, 128-155
U.S. Department of Labor, 9, 127
    Alphabetically by state, 128-155
U.S. Occupational Safety & Health Admin., 127
    Alphabetically by state, 128-155
Utah, 152
Utilities, 83

V

Vermont, 152
Viability, 99-107
Virginia, 153

W

Washington, 153
West Virginia, 154
Wisconsin, 154
Workman's Compensation, 92
Wyoming, 155

Y

Yellow pages, 115

Z

Zoning, 7
Zoning commission, 8, 10
ZONING, LABOR LAWS, &
    LICENSING, 5-10

OTHER BOOKS

by

LINDA PINSON & JERRY JINNETT

1. OUT OF YOUR MIND...AND INTO THE MARKETPLACE

A step-by-step guide for starting and succeeding with a small or home-based business. Takes you through the mechanics of business start-up and provides you with an overview of information on such topics as copyrights, trademarks, and patents, legal structures, financing, and marketing.

2. ANATOMY OF A BUSINESS PLAN

Will enable you to research and write your own business plan. This book is designed to take away the mystery and help you to put together a plan that will both satisfy a lender and enable you to analyze your company and implement changes that will insure success.

AUTOMATE YOUR BUSINESS PLAN — Business Planning Software

3. MARKETING: RESEARCHING AND REACHING YOUR TARGET MARKET

A comprehensive guide to marketing your business. This book not only shows you how to reach your target market, but gives you a wealth of information on how to research that market through the use of library resources, questionnaires, etc.

4. RECORDKEEPING: THE SECRET TO GROWTH & PROFIT

Basic business recordkeeping both explained and illustrated. This book is excellent if you are new to business recordkeeping or if your records are in trouble. It is designed to give a clear understanding of small-business accounting by taking you step-by-step through general records, development of financial statements, tax reporting, the development of a recordkeeping schedule, and financial statement analysis.

These books are available through your bookstore or directly from the publisher, **OUT OF YOUR MIND...AND INTO THE MARKETPLACE™**

OUT OF YOUR MIND...AND INTO THE MARKETPLACE™
13381 White Sand, Tustin, CA 92680
(714) 544-0248